more

When a Little Bit of the Spirit Is Not Enough

D1622941

Alan Kraft

Author *of* Good News for Those Trying Harder

To Craig —
Thanks for your ministry
to The Body of Christ. May
you experience more of
God's Spirit in every facet of
your life &
ministry!

JOSHUA
LUKE
PRESS

John 7:37

Produced and packaged by The Michael Thomas Group
www.themichaelthomasgroup.com

—◊—

*This book is dedicated to my friends and fellow journeyers
at Christ Community Church.
What a privilege it is to experience the Spirit with you.*

Endorsements for *More*

—m—

Alan Kraft authors a thought-provoking work on a traditionally divisive subject, providing a grace-filled and honest interpretation of historically difficult scriptural passages. No matter what your current position is regarding the Spirit, I would highly recommend *More* to drive you deeper into a biblical understanding of the person, role, gifting, and work of the Holy Spirit of God.

Jason Elam,
Author and former kicker,
Denver Broncos

I highly recommend Alan Kraft's new book, *More*. In it, Alan takes us back to the Bible to see what it means to cultivate an intimate relationship with the Spirit. You need to read this book, and so does your pastor. Lighten up! The Holy Spirit is our friend to be embraced and not a foe to be avoided. I'm putting this on my "Must Read" list for our whole ministry.

Alan, thank you for your down to earth and very biblical work on the Holy Spirit and how He wants to revolutionize our lives. We all need More!

Tom Doyle, Vice President, e3 Partners,
Author of *Dreams and Visions-Is Jesus*
Awakening the Muslim World?

We live in an age that longs for the intrusion of the supernatural. Tragically, many followers of Jesus have given up on the idea of the supernatural in favor of muddling through until they get to heaven. What Alan Kraft does in his latest book, *More*, is to show us how the third member of The Trinity — The Holy Spirit — longs to bring heaven to us in the ordinary and everyday. Written on biblical bedrock, with a pastor's heart, Alan shows us that the Holy Spirit is a person with whom we can cultivate intimacy; he shows us how to recognize and listen to the voice of the Spirit; and most importantly he shows us how to live filled with the power of the Spirit so that muddling through until heaven is inconceivable! If you are hungry for MORE of God, this book will change your life and the way you live out your faith. Really.

Michael John Cusick,
Author of *Surfing for God*,
Founder of Restoring the Soul

Years ago, as a young woman, God gave me an intense desire for complete abandonment to the Holy Spirit, longing to live an ordinary life in an extraordinary way. That prayer was answered and decades of fruitful ministry have resulted. Pastor Alan Kraft's carefully crafted, theologically sound, life-tested book *More* has come to me at a time when I had forgotten some of the intensity of that always-hard-to-explain spiritual experience.

What I love about Kraft's approach is that it is not doctrinaire. It is not argumentative. It is instead tender in its understanding that we as humans experience God in different ways — and that this is the beauty of the Body of Christ. I applaud this work. It is a book on the role of the Holy Spirit designed for every heart that is crying, "More!"

Karen Mains,
Author and Director of Hungry Souls

Alan Kraft has written a very helpful and thought-provoking book. It's a clear, well-researched, and incredibly practical approach to an often controversial subject. Odds are you won't agree with everything he says—I'm not sure I agree with it all. But I can guarantee you that your walk with God will be richer, more intimate, and more powerful if you take the time to carefully consider and then apply the important things he has to say. Some of them will be life changers.

Larry Osborne, Author and Pastor
North Coast Church, Vista, CA

Probably the greatest need in the Church today is to have a fresh outpouring of the Holy Spirit. And yet scripture teaches it's the responsibility of every Christ follower to steward our heart to be hungry and open for the work of God the Holy Spirit in our life. In his book *More*, Alan Kraft does an excellent job describing what happens when a Christ follower enjoys the filling and fellowship of the Holy Spirit.

Gerard Long,
Executive Director, Alpha USA

Are you interested in experiencing more of the Holy Spirit in your life? If so, *More,* by Alan Kraft, is just the book for you. With a clear, creative, and captivating writing style, Alan takes you on a thought-provoking and biblical journey into a deeper and more empowering understanding of the person and work of the Holy Spirit, leaving you only wanting more, more, more!

Arron Chambers, Pastor and Author of
Devoted: Isn't It Time To Fall More in Love with Jesus?

Alan has written a book that will help normal people seek and experience the power and the presence of the Holy Spirit. Far too many have been hurt by the excesses of well-intended teachers and preachers. His balance and honesty are really refreshing and helpful for anyone seeking an intimate life with God. If you've wanted a deeper life with the Holy Spirit, but don't want to be weird, this is the book for you.

Jay Pathak, Co-author of
The Art of Neighboring **and**
Senior Pastor of Mile High Vineyard Church

I regularly meet Christ followers who long for *more of Jesus* in their lives. If that is true of you, this book will help you get there through understanding the amazing role that the Holy Spirit wants to play in your life. Understanding His ministry to us can revolutionize our lives. I heartily recommend this book to all who are on the journey of knowing God better.

T.J. Addington, Senior Vice President,
Evangelical Free Church of America,
Leader of ReachGlobal,
Author of *Leading from the Sandbox*

God has given us so much more than a rulebook. He's given us Himself! In *More*, Alan Kraft skillfully guides us through both biblical and practical illustrations, calling us to live with greater expectancy in our relationship with God the Spirit. Solid, biblical, encouraging ... and doable!

Brad Brinson, Senior Pastor,
Two Rivers Church, Knoxville, TN

Alan Kraft's newest book, *More*, deserves to be read by everyone who desires to experience all that the Father has for them in Christ. Grounded in the principles of Scripture, this book merits your thoughtful consideration.

William J. Hamel, President,
Evangelical Free Church of America

Alan Kraft's latest book is a wonderful guide for anyone who is longing for MORE of God's empowering presence. Alan gently and maturely addresses topics such as listening prayer, healing, and prophecy without the eccentricity that so easily plagues these subjects. Thank you, Alan, for your pastoral heart in guiding those of us who long for more of the Spirit.

Kevin J. Navarro, Senior Pastor of
Bethany Evangelical Free Church and
Adjunct Professor at Denver Seminary

Alan's book brings insightful and practical relevance to the power of the Holy Spirit working in the everyday life of the believer. His language activates believers to step into fullness of what is accessible to every one of us! What an incredible tool for the body of Christ in this season!

Sean Feucht,
Author, Songwriter,
and Founder of Burn 24-7

Whether you are shy, skeptical, or currently experiencing an intentional relationship with the Holy Spirit, this book offers something for everyone. Alan offers practical and biblical insights into the joys and power of being aligned with God's activity through relationship with the Holy Spirit.

Tom Ewing,
Worship Pastor/Ministry Consultant

Alan Kraft has provided an outstanding gift to the evangelical community. He's managed to open up greater possibilities of experiencing the Holy Spirit, and done so with grace, logic, biblical fidelity, humility ... and without fanaticism or "weird-ness." Alan is "one of us" who is open to much MORE from God. Shouldn't we all have that attitude? I highly recommend to you this work as a step toward a Spirit-led life.

Rusty Hayes, Sr. Pastor of
First Evangelical Free Church, Rockford, IL,
Author of *All Things New*

I love this book! In it, Alan Kraft offers a wonderful guide-book for the hungry and weary to see God do what they read about in the Bible. The Bible alone will lead to bibliolatry, but when infused with an experiential relationship with the Holy Spirit, we experience a journey that leads to the very edges of heaven.

Alex Mandes,
Director of Immigrant Mission,
Evangelical Free Church of America

In *More*, Alan Kraft proposes that as disciples of Christ, we employ all the resources that God makes available to us. There is a more intimate and glorious way to live, and Alan shows the way. Why approach the challenge of life and mission with only half of your gifts and power? I pray this book catches on!

Bill Hull,
Author of *Christlike: The Pursuit of*
Uncomplicated Obedience

I really appreciate Alan's approach to the work of the Spirit in a believer's life. This book will open up your heart, challenge your thinking, and motivate you to deeply seek all that God wants to put in you through His Spirit.

Dary Northrop, Lead Pastor,
Timberline Church, Fort Collins, CO

I loved Alan's presentation from the text of the intimate and powerful relationship that the early church had with the Holy Spirit. They heard from Him, obeyed Him, were filled with His presence, and empowered by Him, witnessing miracles that powerfully authenticated the gospel of Jesus. They also experienced the power of the Spirit to transform lives. How wonderful to realize this experience is "normal" to the Christian life. So, with Alan Kraft I say, "Come Holy Spirit!"

Ves Sheely, Superintendent,
New England District Association,
Evangelical Free Church of America

Table of Contents

—ᵐ—

Section Three
Experiencing the Spirit in
Healing and Prayer

Section Four
Experiencing the Spirit's Fullness

Introduction

—⟋⟍—

In the fall of 2007, my Colorado Rockies baseball team was on an incredible winning streak, leading to the National League playoffs and eventually the World Series (which we won't talk about). I convinced my wife that our old 27-inch TV wouldn't do, explaining how we couldn't even see the scores from our couch, unless we used binoculars. I laid it on thick. It worked.

Within hours I brought home a 50-inch, plasma HDTV. I couldn't wait to watch baseball and football on this beauty, so I immediately connected all the cables, sound system, and DVD player. When I finished, I eagerly turned on the set to watch a baseball game ... and was totally disappointed. The picture quality looked as lousy as before, except now it was twice as obvious.

Panicking, I grabbed the remote and started exploring buttons. When I hit the INPUT button, I realized that my input was still set on TV rather than HDMI. One click later, I was singing the "Hallelujah Chorus." I could now see the mustard smear on the face of the guy in the stands eating a hot dog. Incredible!

I possessed all the right equipment. I had correctly connected the HD cable. But I wasn't *experiencing* HD ...

until I discovered the INPUT button. That button enabled me to experience the fullness of what was already mine.

Holy Spirit in HD?

For many Christians, our experience with the Holy Spirit resembles my television incident. We have the right "equipment." We know the Bible verses. We believe in the ministry of the Spirit ... but the "picture quality" of our lives doesn't really reflect the Spirit's activity. We long for more—more of His power, more of His love, more of His healing in our normal, everyday lives. And yet we don't know how to get there. So we end up settling for a "little bit" of the Spirit, rather than the "more" our heart yearns for.

If that describes you, I'm so glad you picked up this book. In it, you will discover a practical and biblical pathway into the exhilaration of an everyday relationship with the Spirit in which you can more deeply experience His love, hear His voice, see His power, and live in His fullness.

As an evangelical pastor, I have seen many abuses and excesses regarding the ministry of the Holy Spirit, but I have also personally experienced and observed in others the joys of a growing relationship with the Spirit. I felt compelled to write this book because of the number of Christians and Christian leaders who long to experience the Spirit more deeply but feel afraid or uncertain about going there. This book will reveal how *you* can experience more of the Spirit ... without being weird.

I'm not interested in theory. You can find other books offering that. I want to provide biblical and practical steps to help you experience the Spirit in real ways. Here's where we're headed:

- In Section One, you will discover how you can experience the Spirit *personally*, cultivating an intimate relationship with Him.
- In Section Two, you will learn from the examples and teaching of Scripture how to listen to and recognize the Spirit's voice, as well as how this can enhance your ministry to others.
- In Section Three, you will discover how the Spirit can energize your prayer life, including practical insights into the ministry of healing prayer.
- In Section Four, you will learn how you can be filled with the Spirit's power in ordinary and extraordinary ways.

Throughout the book you will find several "Holy Spirit Laboratory" exercises, providing opportunities to stop and practice what you are reading. To read *about* the Spirit without *experiencing* Him would be to miss the point. So don't hurry through this book. Allow the Spirit to meet you in these pages.

Also, feel free to study this book with a group of friends. (A study guide can be found in the Additional Resource section at the end of the book.) What better way to learn about the Spirit than to do so in community?

Are you ready to experience more of the Holy Spirit? Let's dive in!

Section One

Experiencing the Spirit Personally

Chapter One

You CAN Experience the Spirit

—ɱ—

When I was a kid, my family had a very normal, unimpressive mutt named Caramel. She was overweight, moved slowly, and had dishwater-colored hair. Like I said … fairly unimpressive to the outside world.

But there was something about Caramel I'll never forget. When taking a car ride, she loved having the window all the way down and leaning out to experience the refreshing breeze. Her face held a look of sheer joy as the wind rushed past. She chose the exhilaration of the wind to the quiet, interior comfort of our vehicle.

That image offers a picture of the invitation God extends to us every day regarding the presence of His Holy Spirit in our lives. Will we slightly open the window of our soul, allowing a "little bit" of the Spirit's activity in? Or will we choose to roll the window all the way down so that we can fully experience the Spirit's exhilarating breeze? This book is for those who realize that a little bit of the Spirit is not enough. You long for a life in which you can experience more of God's love, more of His peace and power, more of His presence in every circumstance.

Jesus longs for us to experience this as well. Check out His amazing promise to us in Luke 11:13. "How much more will your Father in heaven give the Holy Spirit to those who ask him?" More of the Spirit. That's the promise Jesus gives to us. Which raises an obvious question: *Why aren't we experiencing the "more" that Jesus promises?*

We can trot out the usual suspects—busyness, distractions, sin. But if we're honest, we realize our struggle actually has a much deeper root. The joy, the peace, the power promised us in Scripture are all dependent upon our *experiencing* the Holy Spirit. And quite honestly, we're not sure what to do with the Holy Spirit.

We know He's important, given how frequently He's mentioned in the Bible. We know He's an essential part of the Trinity. All that is settled in our minds. What we struggle to understand is how we *experience* Him. What does it look like to lean out the window and experience the Spirit more fully?

Is Experiencing the Holy Spirit a Little Scary to You?

I realize this kind of language may be making some of you nervous. I get that. Attending church as a kid, I heard about the "Holy Ghost" and immediately concluded, *I don't want THAT to get near me.* I wasn't interested in hanging out with a ghost, even if it was holy. For many Christians, our image of the Holy Spirit is this impersonal (and at times scary) "force" that we prefer leave us alone.

In college, I found myself engaged in fairly intense conversations with believers who referred to themselves as "Spirit-filled." These friends insisted I wasn't filled with the Spirit because I didn't speak in tongues.

What a challenging and painful season for me. I deeply respected these guys, but I couldn't help feeling that the Christian world was now divided into two camps—the "haves" and the "have nots." And I was a have not.

For some of us, our hesitance in wading into the reality of experiencing the Spirit hearkens back to similar conversations, where a sincere friend tried to project *their* experience of the Spirit onto us, and in doing so made that particular experience a mark of authentic spirituality. Since we don't do *that*—whatever *that* is—we feel like second-class Christians, forever destined to sit on the bench.

Once, at a worship conference, I walked forward to receive prayer. The person praying for me so wanted me to be "slain in the Spirit" that he kept trying to push me over. In that moment, I discovered a new way to apply the apostle Paul's encouragement in Ephesians 6 to "stand firm."

Most of us probably have similar stories where certain "manifestations" of the Spirit were forced upon us or on someone we know, leaving a distinctively bad taste in our mouths. The problem, however, is that we often throw the baby out with the bathwater. Consciously or subconsciously we conclude, *If THAT is what it means to experience the Spirit, I'm not interested.* We end up settling into a Christianity in which we talk about the Spirit and memorize verses about the Spirit and believe truths about the Spirit, but we rarely if ever actually *experience* Him.

> *We end up settling into a Christianity in which we talk about the Spirit ... but we rarely if ever actually experience Him.*

This describes my Christian life for a number of years. I knew the Bible. I memorized Scripture. I was active in ministry. I fasted and prayed regularly. But below the surface lay a weariness, an emptiness, a dissatisfaction. Even with the discouraging conversations I experienced with my friends in college, my heart felt a longing to know the Holy Spirit better. Over time, that began to happen in a variety of ways, which resulted in a passion to help other Christ-followers experience the Spirit more deeply.

It's Time to Peel off Our Labels

Part of the challenge in writing a book like this and in openly sharing my own personal experience is that many of us operate in fairly neat and tidy theological categories regarding the work of the Spirit. We tend to label people who have different experiences than we've had or who use certain words differently than we do or who attend a church with a different perspective on the

The Spirit does not fit well into our narrowly defined theological boxes.

Spirit. Once we determine what camp they are in, we quickly dismiss them—and unfortunately miss an opportunity to grow in our relationship with the Spirit. The Spirit does not fit well into our narrowly defined theological boxes, often working in ways outside our own experience or personal comfort. We too easily dismiss these experiences simply because they don't fit our categories.

I once listened to a podcast of a Bible teacher discussing the authority of Scripture. When asked about the possibility of people coming to know Jesus through dreams and visions rather than a direct interaction with the Bible, he mockingly rejected the idea, asserting that, "These alleged supernatural experiences are outside of what the Bible teaches."

As I listened, I thought of my conversation not long before with a man in the Middle East who described how he became a Christian: Jesus appeared to him in a vision and called this man to follow Him. He did. He now actively ministers for Jesus among a people very much opposed to Christianity. His story is not unique. I have visited with a number of missionaries in that region who describe how common this phenomenon is.

How easily we can dismiss certain stories that don't fit our theological categories or our experience. Ironically, the Bible offers numerous examples of God speaking to people through dreams and visions. In fact, on the day of Pentecost, Peter stood up and declared this to be one of the marks of the age of the Spirit: "Your young men will see visions, your old men will dream dreams" (Acts 2:17).

We need to be careful, lest we find ourselves on the side of the Pharisees who saw Jesus perform miracles but rejected them because they didn't fit into their theological framework (see Luke 6:6–11 as one of many examples of this). If we truly want to grow in our experience of the Spirit, our hearts need to be open to having our theological boxes expanded — not beyond the principles given in Scripture but certainly beyond our experience. My own Holy Spirit boxes have been expanded numerous times over the years, which makes me hesitant to use labels to categorize the Spirit's activity.

I struggle to find labels that describe my own experience with the Spirit. I don't know what category I fit into. I am a seminary-trained, senior pastor of an evangelical church. I am absolutely committed to the authority and inerrancy of Scripture, to the gospel of Jesus Christ, and to our mission to reach the world. I also frequently pray for the sick. I teach people how to hear God's voice. I sometimes see pictures when I pray for people and will share with them what I sense God saying. I have a personal prayer language that I at times use in my prayer times with God. My life and ministry have been profoundly impacted by two pastors: Tim Keller, a gospel-centered Presbyterian, and the late John Wimber, who founded the Vineyard movement and whose ministry was marked by dramatic manifestations of the Spirit.

For some, this description may cause you to stop reading this book. However, I hope that for many my journey with the Holy Spirit might stir in you a longing to experience Him more fully in your life. I'm not interested in getting anyone to switch camps. I'm not even sure what camp I'm in. I do know that the Holy Spirit has become more real to me over the years and that He wants to do that for you as well.

You Can Enjoy a Relationship with the Spirit

Recently we interviewed a young man for a church staff position. After he effectively answered several ministry-related questions, I decided to throw him what I perceived to be a softball question.

"Tell me about your relationship with the Holy Spirit?" Given that his denomination has historically been open to the work of the Spirit, I assumed this question would be a no brainer.

Silence. "Uh ... well ... He's really important, you know. Um, He ... well, He helps me be a better Christian, I guess ... Is that what you are asking?"

I followed up to clarify but quickly realized this question was no softball question at all. It was a question he struggled to answer. He's not alone. I find that very few Christians feel comfortable talking about their relationship with the Holy Spirit.

Not so for the apostle Paul. For Paul, the Holy Spirit was not a convenient afterthought or a minor theological concept but rather a vital part of his everyday experience. Paul talked about the Holy Spirit the way we talk about a personal friend.

For instance, in a letter to the church at Philippi — a letter Paul wrote from prison — Paul said, "Yes, and I will continue to rejoice, for I know that through your

Paul talked about the Holy Spirit the way we talk about a personal friend.

prayers and the help given by the Spirit of Jesus Christ, what has happened to me will turn out for my deliverance" (Philippians 1:18-19, NIV84). In the midst of dire circumstances, Paul acknowledged the personal help he received from the Spirit.

Or how about Romans 8:26, where Paul declared, "In the same way, the Spirit helps us in our weaknesses. We do not know what we ought to pray for, but the Spirit himself intercedes for us through wordless groans."

Help in weakness. This depicts what a close personal friend would do — offer tangible help in a time of need. Paul felt very comfortable talking about his personal relationship with the Spirit. Clearly this relationship was vital to his Christian experience and to ours as well.

Getting Up Close and Personal

In the New Testament, when someone wanted to describe a significant level of participation or personal engagement, they frequently used a particular Greek word, *koinonia*, which is often translated "fellowship" or "participation" (see Acts 2:42 and Philippians 3:10). In today's terminology, the word *koinonia* describes the difference between watching from the sidelines or playing in the game. Huge difference.

One of my sons is learning to drive. For the first 15 years of his life, he rode in the backseat of a car, oblivious to stop lights, lane changes, and street names. Now that he sits in the driver's seat, he suddenly has a new appreciation for the complexity of automobile transportation. That's *koinonia*—not simply a distant awareness but a personal experience.

In light of this definition, it is fascinating that Paul twice chose this word to describe our relationship with the Holy Spirit. In 2 Corinthians 13:14, Paul declared, "May the grace of the Lord Jesus Christ, and the love of God, and the fellowship (*koinonia*) of the Holy Spirit be with you all." Paul was describing our personal engagement with the Spirit of God.

Similarly, in Philippians 2:1-2, Paul wrote, "If you have any encouragement from being united with Christ, if any comfort from his love, if any fellowship (*koinonia*) with the Spirit ... then make my joy complete by being like-minded, having the same love, being one in spirit and purpose" (NIV84).

Experiencing the Spirit is normal Christianity. Paul realized that unity in relationships depends on every believer experiencing *koinonia* with the Spirit of God—a very real, personal, engaging relationship with the Spirit. For Paul, *experiencing the Spirit is normal Christianity.* This is not for a few select, super spiritual saints. Every believer has this privilege.

Does Jesus Agree?

So how does all of this strike you? Does this stir within you a longing for a deepening experience with the Spirit? If so, great! Keep reading. However, I'm guessing that for others, this kind of talk still makes you a bit uncomfortable. Isn't there a danger that we might be emphasizing the Spirit too much? I'm certainly not arguing for de-emphasizing the Father and the Son, while elevating the work of the Spirit. I am, however, passionate that our relationship with the Spirit aligns with the picture given in the New Testament—where the ministry of the Spirit is essential in experiencing the fullness of the Father and the Son.

In John 14–16, as Jesus explains the reality of His departure, He encourages the disciples to not let their hearts be troubled and to trust Him when circumstances seem dark and difficult. But He actually offers them more than an exhortation to deeper faith. Read the following verses carefully:

> If you love me, you will obey what I command. And I will ask the Father, and he will give you another Counselor to be with you forever—the Spirit of truth. The world cannot accept him, because it neither sees him nor knows him. But you know him, for he lives with you and will be in you. I will not leave you as orphans; I will come to you.   John 14:15–18 (NIV84)

Did you notice what He offers them? He promises to give them "another Counselor." This word translated "Counselor" refers to an advocate, one who comes alongside to assist, to help, to encourage. What's fascinating is that Jesus describes the Spirit as "another" Counselor. This Greek word specifically refers to another of the same kind. In other words, the Spirit that Jesus promises will have a similar ministry as He had among them—with one crucial distinction: "But you know him, for he lives with you *and will be in you*" (John 14:17, my emphasis).

Whereas Jesus' ministry to them had been external— a relationship among people—now the Spirit's ministry to them will be internal; the Spirit of God living in them. Jesus promises them an even deeper experience after He leaves. In fact, notice how Jesus describes this Spirit. "I will not leave you as orphans; I will come to you" (John 14:18). He doesn't say "I will not leave you as orphans; My Spirit will come to you." No. He says, "*I* will come to you."

From Jesus' perspective, the Spirit that would come to live in His followers was Jesus' very own presence! That's why Luke and Paul both speak of the "Spirit of Jesus" or the "Spirit of Jesus Christ" (see Acts 16:7 and Philippians 1:19). The Holy Spirit is the very presence of Jesus in us. You can't get more personal than that.

Recently my dad, my son, and I were heading back home after doing some shopping about an hour away. Unfamiliar with the area, I soon found myself disoriented and uncertain as to the direction to go. Okay ... we were lost.

The Holy Spirit is the very presence of Jesus in us.

At that point the three of us males decided to do something highly unusual for our gender: we asked for directions. Pulling into a car dealership, we found a very helpful young man who knew exactly how to get us home.

"Take a right out of the parking lot," he told us. "Then go left at the railroad tracks. At the next light, take a right and stay on that road and it will get you exactly where you need to go."

It sounded simple enough, but I took notes just in case. We drove out of the dealership ... and within three minutes were completely lost again. The path home wasn't quite as simple as he described. At that moment, I realized what we really needed—that young man in our car. We needed him sitting next to us, guiding us to our destination.

For many believers in Christ, we settle for directions in our relationship with God. We view the Bible as a guidebook, telling us how to live. But it doesn't take long to realize we need more than a list of guidelines to follow. We need the very Person of God living in us — His power, His presence with us. The Spirit enables this to happen.

The Presence of God Lives in You

Not surprisingly, the entire story of the Bible centers around this idea of God's presence with His people. The tabernacle and then the temple were both physical localities in which God's presence dwelt. But in the New Testament, something absolutely glorious happened on the day of Pentecost. God gave His Spirit to every believer in Jesus. Paul later declared this to be the essence of the gospel: "Christ in you" (Colossians 1:27). The very presence of God lives in us. We are now the temple, the place in which God's Spirit dwells.

What an incredible truth! What an awesome reality — the actual presence of Jesus living in you through the Spirit. Not information. Not a map. Not a list of rules to follow. If you have placed your trust in Jesus, this is absolutely true of you. God's very own Spirit lives in you.

So how can we experience more of this Spirit in our lives? That's the question we will explore in the chapters ahead. But before you go there, I encourage you to stop reading and take a few minutes to reflect upon your relationship with the Holy Spirit.

HOLY SPIRIT LABORATORY

On a piece of paper or in your journal, answer the following question:

How would you describe your relationship with the Holy Spirit?

After answering that question, slowly read Jesus' words in John 14:15-18:

"If you love me, you will obey what I command. And I will ask the Father, and he will give you another Counselor to be with you forever—the Spirit of truth. The world cannot accept him, because it neither sees him nor knows him. But you know him, for he lives with you and will be in you. I will not leave you as orphans; I will come to you." (NIV84)

What do you long for your relationship with the Spirit to be like? Be specific.

Take a moment and ask the Father for more of the Holy Spirit in your life.

[If you are uncertain as to whether or not you even have a relationship with the Spirit, please turn to page 211, endnote 1]

Chapter Two

The Essential, Overlooked Ingredient to More of the Spirit

—⁕—

I hate to wait. Whether waiting in a doctor's office, waiting for a light to turn green, waiting for a website to download ... doesn't matter. I don't like waiting. In a matter of seconds, my blood pressure rises, my heart rate increases, and my level of impatience elevates.

Can you relate? How many of us have paid a few hundred dollars extra so that our new computer processor will run faster? Never mind that the actual speed increases a tenth of a nanosecond. We want fast and we want it now.

A *New York Times* article reported that Americans spend roughly 37 billion hours each year waiting in line. This same article identified the emotions we experience while waiting: "stress, boredom, that nagging sensation that one's life is slipping away."[1] Any idea why Disneyland intentionally designs its amusement park lines to wrap around buildings and form winding queues? To hide the length so we won't get as frustrated while waiting. None of us like to wait.

Why is waiting an experience we so desperately want to avoid? It's all about control. Waiting means someone else is in control of my life, my schedule, my time at that moment — and I don't like that. And neither do you. We like to run our lives. We like to manage every minute of our schedules. We like to be God.

In light of our aversion to waiting, I find it interesting and a bit unsettling that when Jesus instructed His followers how they could experience the life-giving power of the Spirit, He offered this initial command: Wait. "Do not leave Jerusalem, but wait for the gift my Father promised, which you have heard me speak about" (Acts 1:4).

Seriously? If I were one of the disciples, I would have been beside myself. "Are you kidding me? Why do we need to wait? The world needs to hear the gospel. Ministry needs to happen. What could possibly be the value in waiting?" Great question. What could be the value in waiting?

The Unintended Benefit of Waiting

A friend of mine went to the hospital thinking he had the stomach flu, only to have the doctors discover two malignant tumors surrounding a section of his colon. They immediately performed surgery, removing the tumors, but then the waiting began. Three days awaiting the pathology results. Excruciating. It's one thing to wait at a stop light or in a doctor's office. It's another thing to wait for news upon which your life depends.

In those circumstances, our waiting highlights the fact that this situation is completely out of our control. We are totally dependent upon someone else to bring the information we need. It's a very humbling place to be. Now granted this is a fairly dramatic example of waiting, but it highlights a significant reason we hate to wait: We don't like being dependent on anyone or anything else. Waiting makes us acutely aware of our need—which is exactly what makes it so spiritually powerful.

When Jesus urged His disciples to wait for the Spirit, notice the first thing He told them: "Do not leave Jerusalem, but wait for the gift my Father promised" (Acts 1:4). In other words, don't leave home without the Spirit. This command highlights the fact that the disciples were not in control of their situation. *They* were not calling the shots; Jesus was. The waiting in Jerusalem speaks of their absolute dependence upon the Holy Spirit. Jesus wanted them to know they could not possibly accomplish the mission on their own. So the command to wait was fueled by an awareness of their need.

This awareness of our need becomes the fertile soil in which the Spirit of God moves most freely. He is not looking for the able, the competent, the perfect, the well-adjusted, the successful, the self-sufficient. Quite the opposite. The Spirit is looking for those who are aware of how much they need Him. Jesus makes this abundantly clear in John 7:37–39.

> Jesus stood and said in a loud voice, "Let anyone who is thirsty come to me and drink. Whoever believes in me, as Scripture has said, rivers of living water will flow from within them." By this he meant the Spirit, whom those who believed in him were later to receive. Up to that time the Spirit had not yet been given, since Jesus had not yet been glorified.

I love the imagery Jesus uses. He likens the Spirit to rivers of living water that will flow from within us. This image vividly describes the fullness God longs to bring to our lives—an experience that refreshes and empowers.

"Rivers" speak of the breadth of what God makes available to us. Not a little drinking fountain or even a stream. We're talking rivers. The imagery communicates limitless amounts of fullness, power, and movement.

Sounds great, but notice the prerequisite Jesus gives for this experience: "Anyone who is thirsty." That's the key that opens the door for a real, life-giving experience with the Spirit. We must be thirsty. In other words, we must be aware of how desperately we need the Spirit of God.

Imagine you had no awareness of thirst in your body. Even though your physical body desperately needed fluid, you wouldn't *Our problem is that* know it. You would eventually *we are not thirsty.* ally die of dehydration, not because of a lack of water supply around you. You would die because you weren't aware of your need. That imagery offers a tragic picture of life without thirst, and even more tragically describes what often passes for Christian growth today.

We love hearing principles for spiritual growth— five steps to a better prayer life, three keys to sharing your faith, four ways to have a successful marriage. The implied message is "Just work at it. You can do this. Here are the steps. Go for it." So we do just that. We make promises. We establish accountability. We commit to a new way of doing life. "I promise I will listen to my wife better. I commit to avoiding porn on the internet. I will make time for prayer with God." All great promises to make. The problem is, they are all built upon an incredibly weak foundation—*our* ability, *our* sufficiency, *our* determination.

Now we of course give lip service to needing the Spirit of God to help us, but in reality, the responsibility for change rests on us. The end result is inevitable failure. We can grit out anything for awhile, but eventually we settle back into the old, comfortable patterns of behavior. We don't lack sincerity or the desire to change. *Our problem is that we are not thirsty.*

We lack awareness of how desperately needy we are—that without experiencing the Spirit's power in these areas, we are toast. "Do not leave Jerusalem," Jesus said. In other words, don't attempt the Christian life without the very real presence of the Spirit empowering you. This life-changing power is promised to those who are thirsty.

What encourages me about Jesus' promise in John 7 is the *continual* nature of the experience. Jesus doesn't describe a onetime event. He is not only talking about initially receiving the presence of the Spirit at conversion. His language articulates a *continual* invitation to us. Anytime, anywhere we are thirsty, we can come to Him and drink more deeply of His Spirit.

How Thirsty Are You?

So how do we cultivate a thirst for the Spirit? How do we foster a deepening dependence upon Him? Paul actually answers that very question for us in 2 Corinthians 12, but let me warn you. His answer is not the answer we want to hear. Instead, we prefer answers like *pray this prayer, read this book, go to this conference*. We want something specific we can do.

But notice how Paul answers this question for us:

> In order to keep me from becoming conceited, I was given a thorn in my flesh, a messenger of Satan, to torment me. Three times I pleaded with the Lord to take it away from me. But he said to me, "My grace is sufficient for you, for my power is made perfect in weakness." Therefore

I will boast all the more gladly about my weaknesses, so that Christ's power may rest on me. That is why, for Christ's sake, I delight in weaknesses, in insults, in hardships, in persecutions, in difficulties. For when I am weak, then I am strong. 2 Corinthians 12:7–10

How's that for a list: weaknesses, insults, hardships, persecutions, difficulties. According to Paul, that's how he experienced a deepening dependence upon the Spirit. This raises an immediate problem for us: we don't really want anything on that list! We don't like to be weak. We don't like to experience hardship or difficulty. But Paul reminds us that all these things provide fertile ground in which we can grow in our experience of the Spirit. Paul actually had the gall to say he *boasted* in his weaknesses; he delighted in them. Why? Because when he was weak, he experienced Christ's presence and power more deeply.

The moment our fourth child was born, we knew something was terribly wrong. Joshua just lay there, listless and unresponsive. He didn't cry. His skin looked different than our other children at birth. The nurses immediately took him to a special unit for oxygen and further testing. That began a journey for our family that none of us would have asked for, and yet we regularly thank God for.

It has been a journey of profound weakness and difficulty. We have seen dozens of medical specialists, tried numerous diets and supplements, read countless books, prayed for healing thousands of times, cried lots of tears, asked God hundreds of questions, felt incredibly helpless and out of control … all the while hoping for a dramatic healing in Josh. Now thirteen years old, Josh has significant cognitive, verbal, and physical delays. These bring to our lives daily challenges as well as many questions about the future.

When my wife Raylene and I look at the past thirteen years through the lens of personal convenience or successfully finding answers, the view looks fairly bleak. But when we look through the lens of the Spirit, the entire view changes. Both of us can attest that the profound weakness we have felt in trying to help Joshua has resulted in a deepening friendship with the Spirit. We share an intimacy in prayer and a spiritual attentiveness to the Spirit's voice that didn't exist before Joshua. In our weakness and difficulty, we have experienced Christ's power resting upon us in a greater way than ever before.

Neither of us would have voluntarily chosen this path, but we are deeply grateful for the spiritual experiences and blessings that have been the direct result. "When I am weak, then I am strong." Paul's words completely alter our paradigm for spiritual growth. Our weaknesses, our failures, the places in our lives where we feel powerless, all provide fertile ground for a deepening experience of the Spirit.

What if we saw our struggle with anger or porn or gossip or greed as a blessing in disguise — a God-given means of reminding us how much we need His Spirit?

Have you thought about your failures and weaknesses in that light? Typically, we see our weaknesses as a liability, something we need to get rid of. But what if we saw them through the lens of the Spirit? What if we saw our struggle with anger or porn or gossip or greed as a blessing in disguise — a God-given means of reminding us how much we need His Spirit?

What if we viewed the challenges in our lives — a difficult marriage, a controlling boss, a wayward child, an ongoing addiction, a recurring anxiety — through a similar lens? Paul boasted in his difficulties and weakness, not because he enjoyed those things, but because they opened a door for him to experience the Spirit more deeply.

HOLY SPIRIT LABORATORY

On a separate sheet of paper, create a list of your weaknesses and difficulties. How do you feel about that list? Discouraged? Overwhelmed? Hopeful?

Now view your list through Paul's lens offered in 2 Corinthians 12:10. For each item, read this passage out loud, filling in the blank with that item.

"That is why, for Christ's sake, I delight in _____ ... for when I am weak, then I am strong."

After each statement, spend a few moments asking the Spirit to rest upon you in the midst of your struggle in that area.

How To Intentionally Be Weak

A few years ago, I journeyed to Uganda on a mission trip with a group from our church. One afternoon we were told that a handful of leaders wanted to meet us, so we drove to a church building in their village, expecting a small group in an informal setting. Upon arrival, we discovered that a hundred people had gathered, waiting hours for us to speak to them. While some pastors would love this kind of spontaneous speaking opportunity, I do not. Being a fairly scripted guy, I like to have things well prepared. I experience recurring nightmares where I am late for a worship service and have forgotten my notes, only to wake up in a cold sweat.

So here I was, living my worst nightmare, and yet a profound sense of peace—almost excitement—descended upon me. I earnestly prayed under my breath for God's Spirit to help me, and He did. I shared a Scripture passage He had brought to my mind moments before. The thoughts and words came to me without having "officially" prepared anything. I experienced the Spirit in a very tangible way—mainly because I was out of my comfort zone and desperately needed Him.

Unfortunately, I find that when I return from a trip like that, I all too easily drift back into my areas of comfort and security—well-planned and scripted speaking engagements. My perception of my need for the Spirit dramatically decreases.

I know I'm not alone in this experience. Years ago, a friend returned home after leading a mission team and described the adventure of getting up every day without having a specific agenda. They prayed in the morning for direction, then went out and connected with people, looking for God to open doors. The stories were amazing. He asked me a simple question: How do we continue in that Spirit-dependent attitude after we return to our everyday lives at home?

It's a great question. Obviously the answer is not a geographical one—that we need to minister somewhere else to experience the Spirit. The issue is dependence. When we place ourselves in contexts out of our comfort zones and choose to minister to people, suddenly our hearts become fertile ground for the power of the Spirit.

Where are you stepping out from your comfort zone? When is the last time you intentionally placed yourself in a situation that required resources beyond what you knew you had? *When I am weak, then I'm strong.* Whether our weaknesses are unintentional (via failures, challenges we didn't ask for, etc.) or intentional (volunteering to do something out of our comfort zone) the result is the same — we are significantly more aware of our need for God's Spirit. That's the context in which He does His best work.

The Beautiful Gift of Longing

Often our weaknesses and desperation open a door for us to experience a significant gift from God: the gift of longing. We long for more of His Spirit, which moves us to seek Him more earnestly. Remember Jesus' invitation from John 7:37? "Let anyone who is thirsty come to me and drink." Those words highlight a vital, relational principle we often overlook: The Spirit waits to be wanted. He does His best work in the hearts of those who long for more of Him.

The first stirrings of my longing for the Spirit occurred during seminary. While knee-deep in classes and papers and lectures and books, God began to stir in my heart a longing for more of Him. I wanted more than book knowledge about God; I wanted to *experience* Him in a real way. Part of this desire resulted from observing a friend who had a very intimate, real relationship with the Holy Spirit. And I wanted that.

The Spirit waits to be wanted.

At the same time, a fellow student introduced me to the writings of John Wimber, who led the Vineyard Movement. As I read some of his books, my yearning for more of the Spirit increased. Wimber's theological perspective intrigued me. He rejected the traditional Pentecostal position that speaking in tongues was *the* evidence of the Spirit's filling, and yet He experienced the Spirit in very real and profound ways. I wanted more. I'll never forget hearing John Wimber share his testimony. In it, he described a season in his Christian life in which he saw the biblical evidence for the Spirit's activity and yet wasn't experiencing it personally. His response? Longing. He began to ask God for more of the Spirit. This was no casual asking. In spite of no immediate answers to his prayers, Wimber continued to ask God earnestly for more. Eventually, God answered that prayer in dramatic ways.

The Spirit waits to be wanted. Are we asking for more of Him?

Is It *Really* Okay to Ask for More of the Spirit?

Now I realize that this kind of language makes some Christians uncomfortable. Over the years, I've heard people assert that it is wrong for us to ask for more of the Spirit. After all, they will say, "He lives in us. The issue is not us having more of Him but Him having more of us." I certainly agree that a critical part of discipleship involves giving the Spirit increasing control of us. However, when we categorically discourage anyone from asking for more of the Spirit, we ignore a significant theme in Scripture.

Look carefully at Jesus' words in Luke 11:9–13.

> So I say to you: Ask and it will be given to you; seek and you will find; knock and the door will be opened to you. For everyone who asks receives; the one who seeks finds; and to the one who knocks, the door will be opened.
> Which of you fathers, if your son asks for a fish, will give him a snake instead? Or if he asks for an egg, will give him a scorpion? If you then,

25

though you are evil, know how to give good gifts to your children, how much more will your Father in heaven give the Holy Spirit to those who ask him?

This passage about asking, seeking, and knocking is familiar to many of us. However, we often fail to realize exactly what Jesus encourages us to ask for. "How much more will your Father in heaven give the Holy Spirit to those who ask him?" Jesus urges us to ask for the Spirit, not simply as our initial response to the gospel. His language describes a *continual* asking, seeking, and knocking. We are to earnestly and persistently ask God the Father to give us more of the Spirit.

Now some may argue that all this talk of asking, seeking, and knocking makes God seem like an insensitive ogre who delights in dangling a carrot in front of us. He just wants to hear us beg. But that is hardly the picture Jesus gives in Luke 11. He specifically uses the analogy of a father giving good gifts to His children to describe how God the Father views us.

As a father, I never tire of hearing my children ask me for good things. The fact that they are asking reveals something important about their heart. To long for and yet never ask reflects a father/child relationship rooted in distance and distrust. God, our loving Father, wants us to ask Him for more of the Spirit. The act of persistent asking reveals a heart truly longing for Him.

Years ago, one of our children expressed an interest in archery. We enrolled him in a Saturday-morning class. Soon, he approached us asking if he could purchase a very expensive archery bow. Rather than immediately saying yes, we chose to wait. Within weeks, he no longer wanted a bow, having lost all interest in archery.

A similar scenario played out years later when he wanted to buy a guitar. This time, however, the longer we waited, the greater his desire became. He kept on asking. Finally we agreed. His earnest and persistent asking revealed a true longing. No wonder Jesus urges us to ask for more of the Spirit. Our asking reveals the depth of our longing.

Other Scriptures also encourage this earnest asking. For instance, in Ephesians 1, Paul prayed for the believers in Ephesus. Look carefully at his prayer: "I keep asking that the God of our Lord Jesus Christ, the glorious Father, may give you the Spirit of wisdom and revelation, so that you may know him better" (Ephesians 1:17). What a fascinating request to pray, especially for believers in whom the Spirit of God already lives. Paul earnestly and continually prays that they would experience *more* of this Spirit who lives in them. From Paul's perspective, more of the Spirit is always available to us. Not only is it appropriate to ask for more; it is critically important to do so.

What Does This Longing Look Like?

Over the years, my heart has been stirred by the stories of men and women who were dissatisfied with what they had experienced of the Spirit. They wanted more … not for selfish gain but for a greater expansion of God's kingdom.

D. L. Moody was one such man. In the late 1800s, he actively presented the claims of Christ to large crowds. One day, en route to another speaking opportunity, an elderly man tapped Moody on the shoulder, pointed a boney finger at him and said, "Young man, when you speak again, honor the Holy Ghost."

More of the Spirit is always available to us.

For the next few months, Moody admits that those words left him unsettled. They wouldn't go away, but instead ignited an awareness of his need. That encounter, along with the prayers of two dear women friends, stirred in Moody a desperate longing for more. In his own words:

> "And there came a great hunger into my soul. I knew not what it was. I began to cry as never before. The hunger increased. I really felt that I did not want to live any longer if I could not have this power for service. I kept on crying all the time that God would fill me with His Holy Spirit … Well, one day, in the city of New York— oh what a day!—I cannot describe it. I seldom refer to it; it is almost too sacred an experience to name. Paul had an experience of which he didn't speak for fourteen years. I can only say that God revealed Himself to me, and I had such an experience of His love that I had to ask Him to stay His hand. I went to preaching again. The sermons were not different; I did not present any new truths, and yet hundreds were converted. I would not now be placed back where I was before that blessed experience if you should give me all the world…"[2]

These stories of D. L. Moody, John Wimber, as well as the believers in the book of Acts remind us that more of the Spirit is always available to us. We never arrive in terms of our experience of the Spirit, as if His work in our lives is somehow capped or that we have all of Him.

HOLY SPIRIT LABORATORY

Before you continue this chapter, take a few minutes and reflect upon Jesus' words in Luke 11:13: "How much more will your Father in heaven give the Holy Spirit to those who ask him!" Read them slowly and prayerfully four or five times. Let them stir in your heart a longing for a greater experience of the Spirit.

Now take a moment and ask your Heavenly Father for more of the Spirit. Build into your prayer life this specific prayer, continually asking, seeking, and knocking for God to give you more.

What If Nothing Happens?

In light of this discussion about longing for more of the Spirit, let me add a few words of caution: Be careful to avoid measuring the "success" of your seeking based on the stories of others. The Spirit's ministry never operates according to formulas. *This is not about getting results; it's about relationship.* His answer to your earnest prayer will most likely look very different than His answer to another person's similar prayer.

Also, don't be discouraged or disappointed if you don't see any immediate or dramatic results when you begin asking. This is not about getting results; it's about relationship. Something spiritually powerful happens *in* us as we ask, seek, and knock. Our desire and dependence upon the Spirit increase, both of which He longs to see happen in our lives. So don't despise the waiting. Don't let it discourage you. Instead let it increase your desire for God.

My own experience of the Spirit has very much been a journey involving seasons of waiting, of longing, of asking, of wondering ... along with periodic seasons of increased activity and the Spirit's evident work. Even though I wish there was a neat and tidy formula for how to "flip the Spirit switch," He never works that way.

In John 3:8, Jesus describes the Spirit as being like the wind. You don't know where He comes from or where He is going. You can't put Him in a box. But you can set your sail so that when He chooses to move, you are right there, open and available to whatever He wants to do in and through you. That sail is set in our hearts as we long for Him and earnestly ask for more of Him.

Recently I enjoyed the privilege of visiting Israel for the first time. It was a 50th birthday bucket list trip for me. On trips like that where you visit multiple sites each day, you can easily find yourself in tourist mode—getting this photo, seeing this site. Near the end of the trip, we stood on the southern steps to the Old City of Jerusalem, the very steps that Jesus walked on His way up to the temple.

Our guide explained that many believe this was the actual spot where Peter preached to the crowds in Acts 2, after the Spirit had been poured out so dramatically. Are you kidding? Here I was, standing on that very spot. Suddenly, my tourist desire to get a picture took a back seat to a deeper desire.

As the group prepared to leave, I quietly asked one of our tour guides (who is also a church planter in Israel) if he would pray for me that I might experience more of the Spirit's power in my life. A huge smile spread across his face as he eagerly agreed. He said, "In all my years of doing tours, no one has ever asked me to do this. I would love to."

So we stood there arm in arm—a church planter and a senior pastor—praying for each other to experience God's Spirit more deeply. That moment was a highlight of my trip and a reminder to me that it's okay to ask for more of the Spirit. More than okay, it's something Jesus and Paul urge us to do. No matter how long we have walked with Christ, there is always more of the Spirit available to us.

Chapter Three

Loved ... Period!

—m—

One evening I watched a television show called *Chopped*. I'm not really into cooking shows but within minutes, I was hooked. In the show, three chef contestants are given a small box of varied foods—like clams, an artichoke, cinnamon, and popcorn. When the 30-minute timer starts, they rush to prepare a gourmet dish using every item in the box. Three judges then taste whatever the contestants prepared, choosing which of the chefs to "chop" from the show. Brutal.

Isn't that the way life feels sometimes? It hands us a box of "stuff" (a variety of circumstances, abilities, emotions, challenges). The clock starts and off we are running, trying to make all this stuff look as good as possible to the world around us. We desperately want to prove that we have worth and value, that we have what it takes.

This stressful, performance-obsession takes its toll. Many Christian counselors assert that the majority of all the internal struggles experienced by their clients would vanish if they understood in the depth of their being one critical reality: God loves them. Period.

Why do we obsess over how we look or how much money we have in the bank or how well our children perform at school or athletics? Why do we so often struggle with addictions to food or gambling or shopping or work or alcohol, etc.? Often these addictions/ obsessions are rooted in a gnawing sense within—that we are not okay. We are not acceptable. So we escape into various activities that seem to feed this need in our soul for affirmation and acceptance. Never mind that they never truly satisfy. We are on a desperate search for love ... in all the wrong places.

The Spirit's Job Description

Even though the world can't satisfy this longing, God provides a way for this need to be met in us. Check out Paul's words in Romans 5:

> Therefore, since we have been justified through faith, we have peace with God through our Lord Jesus Christ, through whom we have gained access by faith into this grace in which we now stand. And we boast in the hope of the glory of God. Not only so, but we also glory in our sufferings, because we know that suffering produces perseverance; perseverance, character; and character, hope. And hope does not put us to shame, because *God's love has been poured out into our hearts through the Holy Spirit*, who has been given to us. Romans 5:1-5 (my emphasis)

Notice the Spirit's job description: To pour out God's love into our hearts. This phrase "pour out" refers to an abundant lavishing of God's love within us. How awesome is that? The Spirit helps us experience the love of God, not simply as some cognitive truth we recite in our minds. Paul describes a real experience, so that we know in the depth of our being that we are loved ... period. Unconditional acceptance and affirmation—the very things our hearts long for.

Is This Love Sappy or Real?

Now I realize that to some, this "love" talk sounds like sappy sentimentality or perhaps new age mysticism. But notice the *basis* for the love God gives: "Therefore since we have been justified through faith, we have peace with God through our Lord Jesus Christ." The only reason we can have peace with God (i.e. experience a love relationship with God) is because of what Jesus has done for us. The moment we place our faith in the work of Christ on the cross, we are "justified." In other words, completely accepted by God, forever forgiven of all sin. Amazing.

> *Although we have received this gift through Christ, we struggle to actually live as beloved, forgiven people whom God accepts.*

But here's our problem. Although we have received this gift through Christ, we struggle to actually *live* as beloved, forgiven people whom God accepts. Instead, we wrestle with insecurity, addictions, anxiety, etc. We know the truth about the gospel of Jesus but are not *experiencing* it.

Enter the Holy Spirit. God gives us the Holy Spirit to make this amazing love real to us. How? Look carefully at the language Paul uses: "And hope does not put us to shame, because God's love has been poured out into our hearts through the Holy Spirit."

Shame. Shame is that "voice" within that continually communicates that something is wrong with us. It shouts at us in our failures, *You jerk. How could you do that? God couldn't possibly love you. And to think, you call yourself a Christian.*

Even in our successes, shame whispers lies into our soul, *If they knew what you were really like, you wouldn't get this award.* Or *This is good but it's not good enough. You gotta keep this up.* Shame is an insidious and constant enemy that hinders our ability to experience the love of God through the Spirit. So how do we turn down the volume of shame in our hearts and turn up the volume of the Spirit? By welcoming the presence of the Spirit into our places of shame and failure.

The Spirit Wants to Be With You ... Stink and All

Too often, we approach our sin and brokenness by trying hard to clean ourselves up so God can love us again. But that's not how the gospel works. Because of the cross, God's love is already ours. Nothing can change it. Nothing can remove it ... not even our sin. As I explain in my first book, *Good News for Those Trying Harder*,

> The gospel says that when Jesus died on the cross, He took *all* of our sin upon Himself—not some of it or most of it. All of it. Not only that, as Jesus hung on the cross, He experienced the horror of absolute separation and isolation from God, crying "My God, my God, why have you forsaken me?" (Matt. 27:46). At that moment, God the Father turned His face away so that we wouldn't have to experience that ever again. Jesus bore our shame so that we would never have to be ashamed before God again. Jesus experienced distance and alienation from God so that we would never have to be distanced and

alienated from God again. That, my friends, is incredible news.

One morning I was exercising on our elliptical cross trainer in the basement. There's a good reason it's in our basement — I sweat a lot and freely spread a stinky aroma. My older children have learned to avoid the area for at least an hour after I'm done. While I was sweating away one morning, my youngest son, Joshua, came downstairs and started to play video games on his Wii. As I mentioned earlier, Joshua is cognitively and verbally delayed, having been diagnosed with autism and apraxia. Even though he struggles to communicate with words, he uses various other means to get his message across. That morning, God expressed a message to me through Joshua.

Having just finished my thirty minutes of cardio, I was dripping with sweat and stink. While the rest of my family would run for cover, Joshua looked at me, smiled, and then patted the seat beside him. He wanted me to sit next to him and play Wii.

"Josh, I'm really sweaty and stinky," I said to him. "Can I take a shower first?" But he kept patting the seat with his hand. He wanted me to be there with him, stink and all. So I joined him on the floor, and we played a video game together.

That's a picture of the Spirit's counterintuitive work in our hearts. In the midst of our stinky behaviors — our failures, our shame — everything within us feels the need to keep God at a distance. After all, we messed up. Surely He doesn't want anything to do with us, for awhile at least. But the Spirit pats the seat next to Himself, saying to our soul, "I want to be with you, stink and all. I want you to know that I love you. Let Me clean up that smelly area of sin in your life. I am here. My love for you has not changed in the least."

Are You an Employee of God?

Later in the book of Romans, Paul unpacks this ministry of the Spirit even further.

> For those who are led by the Spirit of God are the children of God. The Spirit you received does not make you slaves, so that you live in fear again; rather, the Spirit you received brought about your adoption to sonship. And by him we cry, "Abba, Father." The Spirit himself testifies with our spirit that we are God's children.
>
> Romans 8:14–16

Paul explains that the Spirit not only lives in us; He also gives us a new identity. Our old identity was that of a slave. Given the nature of slavery in that day, a more culturally accurate word for us would be "employee." You know what it's like to be an employee. You are there to meet the expectations of the boss. If you do, you get paid your due. If you don't, you get reprimanded or fired. The environment is fear-based.

The Spirit not only lives in us; He also gives us a new identity. Many Christians live as employees of God. Their spiritual experience with Him is rooted in fear. Fear of not doing enough, not being good enough, not jumping through the hoops well enough. The impact on our lives is huge.

I recently visited with a friend who struggles with pornography and with experiencing an authentic, loving connection with his wife. He described how he grew up in a Christian home where, in his head, he knew his parents loved him because they often said, "We love you." But in his heart, he felt that if he didn't perform, his parents didn't really *like* him very much. Sports became a context in which he most often experienced this dichotomy — "We love you. Now go out there and be aggressive." Love plus some requirement.

As an adult, he admitted that he perceives God in a similar way — as the frustrated parent yelling "encouragement" from the sidelines, rather than a smiling parent who delights in his son ... no matter what. No wonder porn became a very powerful pull in his life. In pornography, he tastes an "intimacy" that requires him to do nothing in order to be accepted and loved. It's a false intimacy that never satisfies and often leads to deepening addiction — but it feels real at the time. In porn, he momentarily escapes from his perception of God the disappointed parent. His story is the story of many of us men. We long to be loved, to be delighted in simply for who we are rather than for what we do.

Women also experience this deep feeling of insecurity and fear of being unloved, as they measure themselves by the world's standard of physical attractiveness. Magazine covers, television shows, movies all reinforce this value system. Either way, our souls all too easily embrace the following shame-filled message: *the only way to get the love we crave is to perform or look a certain way.* This inevitably leads to various destructive behaviors. It's all "old identity" stuff. So how do we break free from these old patterns and embrace our new identity? That's actually a crucial part of the Spirit's ministry to us.

The Abba Cry

In Romans 8:15, Paul describes how the Spirit helps us live in this new identity. Look again at this amazing verse:

"And by him we cry, 'Abba, Father.'" (Romans 8:15). That word "Abba" describes how children would address their dad. Not "Father," but rather "Papa" or "Daddy." Imagine a little girl sitting on her dad's lap, or a teenage boy receiving a bear hug. That's Abba. It speaks of closeness and love. Now notice who helps us experience this love: "*By him* we cry, 'Abba Father.'" The Spirit enables us and moves us to know God as our loving Abba. The Spirit makes this love real to us.

For some, the idea of experiencing God in this way is extremely difficult, given their experience with their earthly father. Perhaps he was distant or abusive or absent. Those negative perceptions and experiences run deep in their souls. They cannot simply turn them off like a light switch. But here's the good news—God has given us the Spirit to help us grow in our experience of Him as Abba. He actively works to make that happen.

God has given us the Spirit to help us grow in our experience of Him as Abba.

Deeper than your drivenness, deeper than your insecurity, deeper than your addiction, is a longing to be loved just the way you are. The Holy Spirit knows of this longing and wants to help you direct that longing to your Abba Father. "By him we cry Abba." Let Him move your heart in that direction. In the midst of your failure, your insecurity, your anxiety, your anger, let your Heavenly Father hold you and love you just the way you are.

The Spirit's Whisper

So earnest is the Spirit in His desire for us to experience this new identity as beloved children of God that He takes an active role in this process. "The Spirit himself testifies with our spirit that we are God's children" (Romans 8:16). To testify means to give evidence for something that is true. God the Spirit continually reminds us of our new identity. He repeatedly whispers to our souls, *You are Mine. You are loved. Nothing can ever separate you from this because you are My son/ daughter forever.*

What an incredibly powerful and much-needed ministry in our driven, performance-oriented hearts. To actually hear God continually and personally remind us of our new identity as His beloved children. How well are we hearing that whisper?

One of the activities that helps me better hear the Spirit's loving words is worship. When I was in seminary, God began to stir in my heart a deepening desire to experience the Spirit. For years, my relationship with God was rooted in insecurity and fear, which resulted in a spiritual drivenness and joyless discipline. I hungered for more than wooden obedience. I wanted more of Him.

In my asking and seeking, a friend gave me a worship music cassette tape. The songs were simple and yet were directed to God, expressing love for Him and embracing His love for us. As I listened, the Spirit of God began to touch some places in my heart with His love—places that had been hidden behind a veneer of spiritual performance. Ever since, God has often used worship music to help me experience the love of the Spirit and hear His gentle words of affirmation.

God the Spirit continually reminds us of our new identity.

Several years ago during a discouraging season in my life, I was driving in my car and listening to some worship music. A song came on that spoke very simply about God's love. I had heard the song dozens of times before, but this time, the words penetrated my heart. I began to weep as God's Spirit poured His love into my heart. This wasn't something I was looking for or trying to experience — but God met me in a tender way. I'll never forget it.

People often come up to me after a worship service and, with some embarrassment, describe how they frequently find themselves crying throughout our service. They don't know what's happening to them. I quickly allay their fears, letting them know that the Holy Spirit is pouring out His love into their hearts in a tangible way.

HOLY SPIRIT LABORATORY

Take a few minutes and listen to a favorite worship song that focuses on God's love. As you listen, open your heart to the presence of the Spirit. Imagine yourself being held in His strong, loving arms. Let the Spirit in you cry, "Abba, Father."

Experiencing His Presence in Prayer

Even Jesus needed this divine whisper reminding Him of His identity. In Luke 3:22, Jesus began His public ministry by being baptized. The moment He came out of the water, God the Father spoke. Given that this marked the beginning of Jesus' ministry, we might expect these words to be directional in nature — "Jesus, here's the plan. First go here and do this. Heal the sick, preach the kingdom." But notice what the Father actually said: "You are my Son, whom I love. With you I am well pleased."

This occurs *before* Jesus had done any official ministry, before He had performed any miracles, before He had gone to the cross. God the Father wanted Jesus to know without a doubt that He was His beloved Son ... period. Not coincidentally, this affirming voice from heaven comes as the Holy Spirit descends upon Jesus. Even in the life of Jesus, the Spirit actively reminded Him of His identity as a beloved Son.

Fast forward to Luke 11, where the disciples ask Jesus to teach them to pray. Jesus gives them a pattern of prayer known as the Lord's Prayer. What's fascinating is how Jesus teaches them to begin their prayer: *Our Father*. Anytime we pray, Jesus wants us to begin by reminding ourselves of our identity as beloved sons and daughters of God.

A few years ago, I began to use the Lord's Prayer as a regular pattern to guide my experience of prayer (In chapter 10, I describe this in more detail). I always begin *God the Father wanted Jesus to know without a doubt that He was His beloved Son ... period.* my prayer time where Jesus began His—"Our Father." I take a few minutes to focus on God the Father's love for me. Sometimes I quietly rest in His love, tuning my heart to His presence. Other times, I express this love to Him, "Abba, Father, thank You for loving me just the way I am. Thank You that Your love for me does not depend upon my looks or my performance or the size of the church I serve. I rest in Your love."

This simple practice enables the Spirit to regularly reinforce my new identity by whispering to my soul the truth of God the Father's love for me. I need that reminder because my heart often loses sight of this truth. An angry email from someone in the church, an impatient exchange with one of my children, a meeting with other pastors in which I compare myself to them ... any number of things can cause me to lose sight of my status as God's beloved child.

A friend of mine oversaw a very large construction project at work. One day, his father dropped by, so my friend eagerly showed him around to see the new construction. During this impromptu tour, he felt a longing in his heart for his dad to say, "I'm really proud of you, son." It didn't happen. In fact, he had never heard his dad say those words. The next morning when my friend spent time with the Lord in prayer, God brought to mind that memory from the day before. The Spirit whispered to my friend's soul, "I'm proud of you, My son." It was just what his heart needed to hear.

When Deeper Healing Is Needed

Over the years I have discovered that sometimes our difficulty in grasping this new identity as beloved children is rooted in some pain in our past — when the words or actions of someone wounded our hearts. That pain can subconsciously create a barrier in our hearts, making it difficult to embrace our new identity. In these situations, the Holy Spirit can help bring healing.

Not long ago, I was on a prayer team ministering to a woman. She told us, "I feel relationally disconnected from my husband and children, and even my relationship with God."

As we listened to her share, one of our team members said, "It feels to me that your heart has been removed from feeling much of anything." She agreed, then added, "But I don't know why that is the case."

Sensing this might be rooted in a painful memory, we stopped and asked God for help. "Holy Spirit, if there is a painful memory at the root of this, we ask You to bring to Susan's mind that memory."

We waited for a few moments, and then Susan began to describe a memory. "I'm about four years old and am walking to get the mail with my stepdad. I'm barefoot and the sidewalk is extremely hot. As I tried to walk on the hot pavement, my stepdad got irritated with me and pushed me on the back of my head. I fell face first into the pavement and ended up getting a bloody nose. My stepdad did nothing to help me."

As we processed this memory with her, we discerned that in that moment, her little four-year-old heart embraced a very clear message: "You have to look out for yourself. Your parents don't care that you feel pain or hurt. You've got to buck up and go it alone." As a result, she subconsciously began to live her life being protective, not trusting or being vulnerable.

Often in our pain, we embrace lies like, *I'm alone,* or *No one loves me.* We make vows such as, *I'll never trust anyone again,* or *It's too painful to admit need so I'm not going to let anyone know what I'm really feeling.* These are not conscious decisions. Instead, they're instinctive and protective responses to pain.

> *The Spirit can help us encounter Jesus' love in the midst of our painful wounds from the past.*

Unfortunately, these subconscious wounds, lies, and vows stay with us into adulthood, as was the case with this woman.

So we walked her through a Spirit-directed prayer process which brought to light the pain of the memory, enabled forgiveness to be extended to her stepdad, broke the vows and lies she believed as a result of the incident, and then invited Jesus' presence into that memory, asking Him to do whatever He wanted to do. (I explain this process in detail in the Additional Resources section page 193).

As we waited, she saw in this memory Jesus picking her up from the pavement and carrying her back to her house. He held and comforted her, while cleaning up her face. Then He told her how much He delighted in her and loved her.

How different from the message she had carried in her heart for years. The Spirit can help us encounter Jesus' love in the midst of our painful wounds from the past, breaking the lies we believe and freeing us to live differently. As Scripture says, "Perfect love drives out fear" (1 John 4:18), and "You will know the truth and the truth will set you free" (John 8:32). The Spirit longs to do both of those in our lives.

The Love Journey

Experiencing God's love is a journey. Paul asserts in Romans 8:16 that the Spirit *continually* whispers to our spirit that we are God's children. We need that continual whisper because often our default response to life is performance, perfection, protection, hiding, giving up, etc. We need the Spirit reminding us — through whispers, worship, prayer, healing, community, or any number of other ways — that our Abba Father indeed loves us, no matter what.

I love how Jesus, on the night before His crucifixion, described to His fearful followers the promised ministry of the Spirit: "And I will ask the Father and he will give you ... the Spirit of truth ... I will not leave you as orphans. I will come to you" (John 14:16–18). What is more vulnerable than being an orphan, removed from the love that you are naturally designed to experience?

But Jesus says, because of the Spirit, that is not our experience. We are not left alone as orphans, separated from the love we were created to experience. He is with us. We are His beloved sons and daughters. The Spirit makes these truths real to us.

When I was in high school, I played on the varsity golf team. Our team had grown up playing lots of golf together as kids, so we were actually pretty good. While we were playing a practice round for the state tournament, I stood on the first tee, preparing to hit my drive. A college tournament had just finished so several "important" people were milling around watching.

Feeling extremely nervous as I stood over the ball, I swung and nearly missed it completely. As the ball dribbled off to my right, my teammates started laughing. In total embarrassment and shame, I wanted to crawl under a rock, but there was no place to hide. As I stood off to the side with my head down, I felt a hand on my shoulder and heard a whisper.

"It's okay, Alan. That was just one shot. Let's go tear it up."

It was my coach who, rather than stand at a distance, met me in my shame and spoke words of life and affirmation to my soul. I'll never forget that.

What an incredible joy to realize that in the midst of our failures, our shame, our drivenness to perform, our fears of rejection, God comes to us in the person of the Holy Spirit. He constantly pours out the love of God into our hearts, whispering to us in the depth of our being that we are beloved children ... always ... forever ... period.

Section Two

Experiencing the Spirit's Voice

—⟋⟋⟋—

Chapter Four

A Closed Mouth and a Yellow Pad

—ɯɯ—

I couldn't wait to make the phone call. For weeks our search committee had prayerfully looked at résumés and done phone interviews, hoping to fill a key pastoral staff position in our church. Now we believed we had our person. With this individual's strong résumé and great interview, he quickly rose to the top of our list. We were eager to fly him out for face-to-face interviews. Hence my phone call that morning, inviting him to do just that.

As I reached to dial the number, I distinctly heard in my spirit, *He's not the one.* I hesitated for a moment, then heard the words again. *He's not the one.* I put the phone down and sat there for a few moments, not sure what to do. My emotions were screaming: "C'mon, God. You've got to be kidding. He HAS to be the one."

In my frustration, I called a spiritually mature leader in our church and told him what had happened. After processing with him, I realized I couldn't proceed as planned. I didn't make the call.

A few days later, I met with the search committee and described what had occurred. They hesitantly agreed not to pursue this individual and instead to keep looking. We later discovered he wasn't as strong a candidate as we originally thought. Our change of direction opened a door to find someone more qualified.

Does God Really Speak to Us in This Way?

This example raises two important questions: *Is God really interested in speaking to us this specifically, and if so, why would He want to?* In Ephesians 1:17, the apostle Paul answers both of these questions for us. "I keep asking that the God of our Lord Jesus Christ, the glorious Father, may give you the Spirit of wisdom and revelation, so that you may know him better."

God is very interested in communicating to us specific details about decisions, about life, about ourselves.

Notice how Paul refers to the Holy Spirit: "the Spirit of wisdom and revelation." The Spirit speaks to us wisdom from God the Father and reveals to us things we wouldn't have known otherwise. Apparently God is very interested in communicating to us specific details about decisions, about life, about ourselves.

Which leads to the second question: Why? Why would He want to speak to us in this way? Paul explains in this same verse, "so that you may know him better." Relationship. This is all about relationship.

I have a habit of people watching when I'm in a restaurant, particularly noticing how a man and woman alone at a table communicate. Recently I observed a husband and wife each on their phone, texting other people. Other couples sit in absolute silence. But sometimes I see a couple fully engaged with each other in communication—eye contact, smiling, perhaps holding hands. Their communication reveals that love is alive in their relationship.

No wonder one of the ways the Spirit helps us grow in our love relationship with God is by communicating with us specifically and personally …

- words that can fill our hearts with joy
- insights that give us wisdom in a decision
- promptings that open doors for ministry to others.

We learn to know Him better as we hear and obey His voice. This experience is not for a select few, but is an essential facet of the Christian life. If you are a follower of Jesus, the Spirit longs to speak to you. So let's explore this incredible privilege that is ours.

Scripture Is the Essential Foundation

The foundation for this experience is the Bible. We learn from the Bible about who God is and what He values. We learn about His ultimate revelation in the person of Jesus and about the work of Jesus on the cross. We learn about how we are to live and what the future holds. As we meditate on and study the Scriptures, the Spirit speaks to us, applying these words to our lives. The Bible is our ultimate authority.

But is the Bible the *only* way God speaks to us? As a young Christian, I was taught that God will never communicate to us outside of the Scriptures; everything He wants to communicate to us is contained in His written Word. I certainly understand why some embrace this perspective. By saying

If you are a follower of Jesus, the Spirit longs to speak to you.

God might speak to us beyond the pages of Scripture, aren't we potentially opening a door for someone to add to the revelation of the Bible?

Not necessarily. One can embrace the absolute authority of Scripture AND also believe the Spirit can speak to us details not contained within the pages of Scripture. These are not mutually exclusive. The *authoritative* Word of God reveals that the Spirit speaks to us as God's children.

The Bible Teaches That Every Believer Can Hear God's Voice

Several Bible passages teach that we can expect to hear the Spirit's voice. For instance, look carefully at Jesus' words in John 16:13, 15:

> But when he, the Spirit of truth, comes, he will guide you into all the truth. He will not speak on his own; he will speak only what he hears, and he will tell you what is to come ... the Spirit will receive from me what he will make known to you.

Jesus wanted His followers to know that the Spirit will communicate with them on His behalf. In John 10, Jesus uses the imagery of a shepherd to describe His relationship with us. A key component of a shepherd/ sheep relationship is the ability of the sheep to hear their shepherd's voice. Jesus applies this to us: "My sheep listen to my voice; I know them, and they follow me" (John 10:27).

The apostle Paul also taught that we can hear the Spirit's voice. We looked earlier at Ephesians 1:17, where he describes the Spirit as "the Spirit of wisdom and revelation." Notice also his teaching in Romans 8:

"Those who are led by the Spirit of God are the children of God ... The Spirit himself testifies with our spirit that we are God's children" (Romans 8:14, 16). From Paul's perspective, the Spirit longs to communicate with us as followers of Jesus.

One of the most powerful articulations of this truth occurs in Acts 2, when the promised Spirit is given to every believer. As Peter stands before the crowd and explains what just happened, he quotes a passage from the book of Joel. Notice the specific activity of the Spirit he highlights:

> These people are not drunk, as you suppose. It's only nine in the morning! No, this is what was spoken by the prophet Joel: "In the last days, God says, I will pour out my Spirit on all people. Your sons and daughters will prophesy, your young men will see visions, your old men will dream dreams. Even on my servants, both men and women, I will pour out my Spirit in those days, and they will prophesy." Acts 2:15–18

Peter declares that, from now on, the Spirit will communicate to us through a variety of means: dreams, visions, prophecy (we will talk about these more specifically in the next few chapters). I love how this passage emphasizes that this privilege of hearing the Spirit's voice is available to *every* believer in Jesus — no matter their gender, age, or social status. Every Christian can experience this joyful reality, because the Spirit now lives in us.

This privilege of hearing the Spirit's voice is available to every believer in Jesus — no matter their gender, age, or social status.

More Than Just Teaching

In addition to the teaching of Scripture, the Bible contains numerous *examples* of people who heard God's Spirit speak to them in specific ways. The list begins on page one with Adam and Eve and continues through the final book, as the aging apostle John hears the Spirit speak. In between are spiritual giants like Abraham, Joseph, Moses, Samuel, David, Elijah, Daniel, Isaiah, Jeremiah, and the apostle Paul. But also included are ordinary people like Jacob, Gideon, Mary and Joseph, Zechariah (the father of John the Baptist), the Magi, Simeon, Anna, Philip, as well as numerous others.

Even Jesus was dependent upon the Spirit's voice. Luke states that Jesus was "led by the Spirit into the wilderness" (Luke 4:1). In Mark 1:35, Jesus awoke early to pray and received specific direction for that day's ministry. All of these examples reveal that the Spirit often speaks to God's people, helping us know how to follow Him in specific ways. One of the most vivid examples of this occurs in Acts 16. Check this out:

Paul and his companions traveled throughout the region of Phrygia and Galatia, having been kept by the Holy Spirit from preaching the word in the province of Asia. When they came to the border of Mysia, they tried to enter Bithynia, but the Spirit of Jesus would not allow them to. So they passed by Mysia and went down to Troas. During the night Paul had a vision of a man of Macedonia standing and begging him, "Come over to Macedonia and help us." After Paul had seen the vision, we got ready at once to leave for Macedonia, concluding that God had called us to preach the gospel to them.   Acts 16:6–10

This passage has always intrigued me. Paul and his companions are traveling throughout Asia Minor, looking for places to share the gospel. As they earnestly attempt to fulfill the Great Commission in a particular location, what happens? The Spirit actually keeps them from preaching there. So they try another spot. Again, same result. Apparently the Spirit has a lot to say about where they do or don't preach. Soon, another door opens and they experience significant spiritual fruit there. Why would the Spirit not want to speak to us in similar ways?

In the example I shared earlier regarding the search for a staff position, the Holy Spirit gave us specific information—information we desperately needed. We already knew from the Bible that we were supposed to fulfill the Great Commission, but we needed help in knowing *how* God wanted that to happen. The Spirit chose to provide those specifics for us.

Now I'm not asserting that the Spirit will communicate such trivial details as which shirt to wear, which way to drive to work, what to have for lunch, etc. That kind of expectation for continual "Spirit-led" living could easily lead to bondage more than freedom. However, very few of us fall into that category. Most of us functionally live with little if any expectation that the Spirit might specifically speak to us about anything. Because of this, we are missing out on something huge. So how can we grow in hearing the Spirit's voice?

What Do You Expect?

Airports can be frustrating places. During a recent trip, I grew impatient waiting several minutes for my luggage at an airport baggage claim. Finally, it was obvious my luggage didn't make it, so I headed to customer service. When the employee heard my name, he said, "Right when you arrived, we knew your bag didn't make it, so I've been paging you on the airport intercom for the last 15 minutes to expedite our ability to help you get your luggage."

They loudly proclaimed my name multiple times on the airport sound system, but I never heard it. Why? Because I wasn't expecting it. I wasn't tuning in to anything they were saying. In a similar way, if we want to hear God speak, we must live with an expectancy that He wants to speak to us. If we don't expect God to speak, we will struggle to hear His voice. Expectations matter.

Some of us suffer from low expectations because of our theological perspective. We have been taught that God no longer speaks in these ways. To remedy this, spend time reflecting on the passages discussed earlier in this chapter. Let the teaching and the examples in the Bible stir your faith. The Spirit really does want to communicate with you!

If we don't expect God to speak, we will struggle to hear His voice.

For others, our past experiences decrease our expectations. Because of our frustrating struggle to hear His voice, we give up on the possibility entirely. I certainly understand. That actually describes much of my Christian life, including several of my years as senior pastor. Fully convinced from Scripture that God still speaks to believers today, I desperately longed for Him to speak to me. My problem was that it never happened to me ... or so I thought.

Just to give you a picture of my level of frustration and desperation to hear the Spirit's voice, a few years into my pastoral ministry, my wife and I drove to a nearby city to hear one of my favorite authors speak. That night John White talked about hearing the voice of God. Several hundred people attended the event. At the end of his message, he asked for a specific response.

"If there is anyone here who feels that they have never heard God speak to them, would you stand?"

I felt my heart pounding in my chest and knew what I must do. I stood, expecting many others to do so as well. That didn't happen. Only three people were standing, including me. There I stood, a senior pastor, openly admitting I never heard God's voice. I felt like crawling under a chair from embarrassment.

In that moment, my two polar opposite perspectives were vividly on display — my theological belief that God does speak to His people and my functional frustration that this never happened to me. While horrifying at the time, that moment began a journey of learning how to better hear the Spirit speak. In that place of frustrated expectancy, I eventually discovered that God had actually been speaking to me all along. I just didn't recognize His voice.

Right-Size Your Expectations

For several years, I thought that whenever the Holy Spirit spoke to me, His voice would be obvious. An unmistakable, audible voice that couldn't possibly be ignored; an HD-quality vision in my mind's eye, one that took my breath away. That's what I expected. That's probably what most of us expect. After all, we live in a culture that constantly communicates to us through vivid HD imagery and unsubtle verbal marketing that's impossible to ignore.

But God doesn't usually speak that way. He doesn't speak to us in the loud, "in your face" manner of our culture. Because of that, we can easily miss His voice. He may be speaking, but we aren't tuned in. I'm reminded of Elijah's example in 1 Kings 19, where he was emotionally and physically weary, desperately needing to hear the Lord's voice.

> Then a great and powerful wind tore the mountains apart and shattered the rocks before the LORD, but the LORD was not in the wind. After the wind there was an earthquake, but the LORD was not in the earthquake. After the earthquake came a fire, but the LORD was not in the fire. And after the fire came a gentle whisper. When Elijah heard it, he pulled his cloak over his face and went out and stood at the mouth of the cave. Then a voice said to him, "What are you doing here, Elijah?"   1 Kings 19:11–13

Wind, earthquake, fire … all very dramatic ways of communicating, but the Lord wasn't in any of those. Then Elijah heard a gentle whisper—a still, small voice. So what does he do? He steps out of the cave he has been in and he stands there, waiting.

This story is instructive in terms of how we can better hear the Spirit's voice. We must right-size our expectations. God usually speaks, not in the dramatic—the lightning bolt from heaven, the mighty wind, the deafening voice—but rather in a gentle whisper, which is easy to ignore. I now believe the Lord had been speaking to me for years. I just didn't recognize His voice. I was expecting the dramatic. He was whispering.

Sometimes We Just Need to Show Up and Shut Up

A friend of mine once heard Brennan Manning articulate the key to hearing God's voice: "Show up and shut up." He does have a point. In Elijah's case, he initially talked to God about all of his troubles (see 1 Kings 19:10).

But when he realized God wanted to speak, Elijah didn't say anything. He just stood there.

I wonder if part of the reason we struggle to hear God speak is that we talk too much. Even when praying with a group of people, we tend to focus on what *we* want to pray. We never stop long enough to listen to the Spirit. What might happen if we did?

A number of years ago, our church needed to make a significant decision that would affect the trajectory of our congregation for decades. Because of our growing attendance, we were maxing out our land-locked, parking-challenged, aging facility. Our church leadership spent several months exploring our options: Relocate to a larger facility? Purchase land on the west side where our city was growing? Remodel our current facility? After much prayerful processing and discussions, we still didn't know what to do.

In desperation I called together our primary leadership team one Saturday morning, gave each a yellow pad and a pen, and said, "For the next 45 minutes, we are going to listen to God.

God usually speaks, not in the dramatic but rather in a gentle whisper, which is easy to ignore.

No praying aloud. No discussions. I want you to listen to the Holy Spirit and write down on the note pad anything you sense He is laying on your heart." This was radical for us. We had talked and discussed and even prayed plenty of times ... but we hadn't ever spent any time listening to the Spirit.

So for 45 minutes, we shut up. After the silence, I asked all the leaders to share what they had sensed the Lord saying regarding this decision. For some, specific Scriptures came to mind. For others, phrases or images sort of "dropped" into their hearts. As each person shared, a few key themes began to emerge. One, we were supposed to stay put and focus on continuing to love the people around us. Two, we sensed that God was already orchestrating a plan that we were going to "fall into."

Believing that God had spoken to us, we stopped worrying about what to do and instead continued to love people. Sure enough, within a few months a plan became clear to us, involving the purchase of five houses to the north of our facility and building a larger worship center. As these plans came to fruition, God indeed began to open doors for greater ministry in our neighborhood and community. And to think: the catalyst for this was a closed mouth and a yellow pad.

How to Increase Our Awareness of God's Voice

Once we right-size our expectations and quiet ourselves before the Lord, how do we tune in to His voice? By cultivating what I describe as *spiritual attentiveness.* When Elijah realized God was speaking in a whisper, he came out of the cave and waited. In other words, he intentionally placed himself in a posture of attentiveness.

When the Spirit speaks, His voice often initially feels like a fleeting thought, something we could easily ignore.

What do we instinctively do when someone is whispering to us? We lean closer. We focus our attention on them. We don't want to miss anything they are saying. That's what spiritual attentiveness looks like — intentionally paying attention to the Spirit's gentle voice, focusing our heart in His direction. This kind of hearing is different than we're accustomed to, because our physical ears aren't involved.

Given the noisiness and busyness of our culture, we often best learn to be spiritually attentive by spending time alone with God in a quiet place—no cell phone, no Post-it-notes screaming for attention, no television or music playing in the background … just silence.

Now let me warn you. At first this will probably be a bit unnerving. Your brain will race a hundred miles per hour. Distracting thoughts will come to mind. Focusing will be difficult. It's okay. That's all normal. We are so accustomed to noise and busyness, that when we stop, our "engine" may continue revving. But don't be discouraged. Over time, with practice, your mind and heart will become more quiet and attentive to the Spirit's whispers.

We hear these whispers by intentionally paying attention to the words, thoughts, ideas, or pictures that the Spirit "drops" into our mind or heart. As I mentioned earlier, we often don't pay attention to these spiritual communications because they are not "shouting" at us like the world typically does. When the Spirit speaks, His voice often initially feels like a fleeting thought, something we could easily ignore. But instead of ignoring it, we must choose to pay attention.

Asking Questions

When I initially tried to grow in hearing God's voice, the experience felt overwhelming and discouraging because of my difficulty in focusing. Thankfully, someone suggested a practice I found extremely helpful: Instead of trying to hear God speak on any subject He chooses, focus your heart and mind by *asking Him a specific question*. Here are a few sample questions that work well[1]:

God, when You look at me, what do You see?

What do You like about me? Why?

When was the last time You laughed over me? Why?

What is one area of my life in which Your love is not fully being experienced?

Rather than being heavy or superficial, these questions help focus our heart on our love relationship with God — which the Spirit loves to communicate to us about (see Romans 8:16). Our goal is learning to hear the voice of our loving Shepherd. He really does want to speak to us, helping us grow in intimacy with Him.

HOLY SPIRIT LABORATORY

In this exercise, you will practice being attentive to the Spirit's voice. Grab a piece of paper and pen, and then find a quiet spot with no distractions. Take a few minutes to quiet your heart. Sometimes it helps to focus on your breathing as a means of bringing stillness to your soul. When your heart is quiet, ask God one of the previously mentioned questions. Then listen for His answer. Write down whatever you hear.

Don't worry about analyzing what comes to mind. Just write down whatever you are sensing. You can evaluate later whether or not it aligns with Scripture. Initially, your goal is to simply tune your heart to hear what the Spirit might say. Ready? Go for it.

So how was the experience? Did any thoughts or words or pictures come to mind? If so, great. If you didn't hear anything, that's okay. Don't give up. We are so accustomed to noise and busyness that initially quieting our hearts can be difficult. With practice, however, you will grow in your ability to tune in to the Spirit.

The examples and teaching of Scripture declare that hearing the Spirit's voice is the birthright of every believer. He loves to speak to His children. What an amazing adventure awaits as we learn to hear His voice.

So what are some of the specific ways God speaks and how do we know for sure it is Him? Those are our topics in the next chapter.

Chapter Five

Is That Really You, God?

—⁂—

S everal months ago I read an article in which a Bible
scholar addressed the topic of knowing God's will.
His approach to decision making was quite simple and
straightforward: God has given us a brain and the Bible.
Why would we need anything else? I certainly understand how this perspective might be appealing. It's
simple, rational, and removes any mystical, weird, or
unclear experiences we could have when trying to hear
God's voice.

What it leaves out, however, is personal interaction
with God. In this approach, God is distant, unwilling
to engage with us in any personal way. The Spirit gets
relegated to little more than a theological concept.

Thankfully, the New Testament offers us a very
different picture, one in which the Spirit regularly
speaks to us. Now I readily admit the messiness that
may occur when we open the door to this possibility.
We need ways to discern whether or not what we are
hearing is God. We may feel foolish when we hear
something that doesn't make any sense to us at the time.

But even with all the messiness, I can't imagine my life without this experience. To hear the Spirit speak opens the door to a wonderful adventure of personal engagement with God.

God Speaks in Various Ways

Part of that adventure occurs when we discover that the Spirit speaks in a variety of ways. The Bible reveals not a one-size-fits-all approach, but rather an incredible diversity in how God speaks. This means we've been given the awesome opportunity to learn how the Spirit speaks to *us*. How wonderfully freeing to realize God may speak to us differently than He speaks to someone else.

In addition, understanding the various means by which the Spirit speaks opens the door for us to hear God in ways we otherwise wouldn't have been attentive to. So let's explore five common ways the Spirit speaks:

- The Bible
- Hearing
- Seeing
- Sensing
- Messengers

The Bible Is God's Foundation for Speaking to Us

The Bible provides the foundational means of hearing the Spirit. As God's primary revelation to us, the Bible is our ultimate authority. Everything we think we hear from God must align with the principles in Scripture. If someone says, "I feel such a peace about my boyfriend and me being sexually involved," or "God told me I don't need to forgive this person who hurt me," we can assert that they are not hearing God. What they are supposedly hearing clearly violates the teaching of Scripture. So the Bible provides an essential filter through which we evaluate what we sense God saying.

However, the Bible provides more than a filter. God *speaks* to us in His Word. He reveals to us His glory. He discloses to us His plan to rescue and redeem humanity through His Son Jesus Christ. He explains to us how to treat others and what holiness looks like. He unveils *Regularly engaging in Scripture helps us grow in listening to the Spirit's voice.* for us the depths of His love and the majesty of His Sovereign power. I could go on and on. The Bible provides our foundation for learning who God is and for Him speaking into our lives. Regularly engaging in Scripture helps us grow in listening to the Spirit's voice.[1]

Hearing

A second way God speaks is through hearing. I'm not referring to an audible voice, but rather a hearing that occurs in our inner being, as thoughts or phrases come to our mind or heart. Our Spirit lab at the end of last chapter provided opportunity for this. In moments of quiet, we may hear a single word or a phrase. A person's name or a Scripture reference may come to mind. We may even hear a song in our spirit. Whatever form it takes, the Spirit reveals to us something that we hear in our inner being.

A great example of this is found in Acts 13, where some church leaders gathered for worship and prayer. "While they were worshipping the Lord and fasting, the Holy Spirit said, 'Set apart for me Barnabas and Saul for the work to which I have called them'" (verse 2). We don't know exactly how they experienced the Spirit's voice, but most likely that specific phrase came to the mind of one or more of those gathered. When shared with the group, they were convinced this was the Lord speaking.

Another biblical example of this is Simeon, an aged and devout Jew to whom the Spirit of God revealed that he would see the Messiah before he died. We are told in Luke 2:27, "Moved by the Spirit, he went into the temple courts," where Jesus and His parents just happened to be. Of course, this was no coincidence. The Spirit spoke to Simeon, moving him to go to the temple at just the right time.

The Spirit doesn't often use a loudspeaker but rather gently drops these thoughts into our heart or mind.

My wife, Raylene, often hears the Spirit give her words or phrases when she prays for people. Not long ago, she prayed for a woman she didn't know well. As she prayed, she heard the phrase, "mother of many." Raylene gently mentioned this phrase to the woman and then offered a brief prayer. She later found out this woman, who is single and doesn't have children, had recently gotten involved in a ministry in Africa, where many of the orphaned children refer to her as Mom. My wife's words spoke volumes to this woman's soul.

I once prayed for a woman for physical healing. As we prayed, I briefly heard in my heart the name "Karen," so I asked her, "Does the name Karen mean anything to you?" With a surprised look on her face, she acknowledged a strained relationship with a woman named Karen. The Spirit wanted her to forgive this woman as part of His healing in her life.

Years ago, as someone prayed for me, the song "Walk Like a Man" started playing in his mind. As he mentioned this to me, I thought of a particular leadership situation

I was facing. I believe the Lord was encouraging me to not be afraid but to lead with courage. These few examples demonstrate how the Spirit may communicate to us through hearing.

Now as we discussed in the previous chapter, we can easily ignore these words, phrases, and Scripture references. The Spirit doesn't often use a loudspeaker but rather gently drops these thoughts into our hearts or minds. I'm guessing many of us have ignored them because they seemed so subtle and even fleeting. We will grow in hearing the Spirit's voice as we practice paying attention to what we are hearing in our inner being.

Seeing

A third way the Spirit speaks is through seeing — not with our physical eyes but rather our spiritual eyes. In this case, we see in our mind's eye a written word or a picture. Biblically speaking, there are two general categories of seeing:

Visions

One type of seeing occurs when we are awake. The Bible refers to this as a "vision." Typically when we think of someone in the Bible receiving a vision, we picture them in a trance-like state, seeing amazing scenes before them. For instance, Peter's dramatic vision regarding the Gentiles (Acts 10) or Isaiah's incredible vision of the throne room of heaven (Isaiah 6).

But Scripture also contains examples of more simple visions. In Acts 16:9, Paul saw in a vision a man saying, "Come over to Macedonia and help us." When the Spirit was poured out upon the church in Acts 2, one of the Old Testament prophecies Peter declared as fulfilled was this: "Your young men will see visions" (Acts 2:17).

Apparently God's people can expect to see visions now that the Spirit has been given.

What significantly changed my experience in this area was when I realized that a vision can simply be a picture God may give to us in our mind or heart as we pray. This might be a detailed, moving picture (which often seems to be the case in Scripture), but it doesn't need to be. Sometimes the Spirit brings to our mind an image or picture.

Until a few years ago, I would have considered it impossible that I would ever see visions. That was something reserved for a select few super-spiritual types. But one day, as I prayed with a young man, I decided to pay more attention to the images that might come to mind. Immediately I saw an image of an old steam engine train. Rather than ignoring this image — which was my typical response — I began to think about it. As I did, the picture became clearer. I saw a winding railroad track headed up a hill and also the engine room in greater detail. What surprised me even more was that I felt like I knew what this picture meant for this person.

A vision can simply be a picture God may give to us in our mind or heart as we pray.

I sensed God saying that the path laid out before this young man would be challenging and difficult (thus the winding track uphill). I also felt the engine room represented the vital importance of this young man stoking the fire of his love for Jesus during this challenging season. I shared all this with the young man and then prayed for him in these areas. He felt genuinely encouraged.

A few minutes after he left, I realized something: I think I just saw a vision! It didn't happen the way I thought it was supposed to — HD, color, vivid imagery — but rather as a fleeting image I typically ignored. By choosing not to dismiss it, the picture became clearer, along with the meaning of the image. That has now happened many times since that first experience.

Not long ago I was with a group of missionaries in an unstructured worship service. While we sang, I quieted my heart to see if the Spirit wanted to communicate anything. Immediately an image of bubble wrap came to my mind. I thought to myself, *What on earth is the significance of bubble wrap?* I nearly dismissed this as my own random brain activity, when a thought struck me. We use bubble wrap when we send something very precious and don't want it to break. Suddenly I knew why that image came to mind. These missionaries were God's bubble-wrapped servants. He wanted them to know He had sent them and wrapped them in His love, because they were very precious to Him.

As the meaning became clear, I began to weep. The Spirit confirmed to my heart His message for these people, which I then shared with them. I certainly could have stood up and told them that God loved them, but the image of being bubble wrapped made that message far more personal and powerful. In a span of three minutes, the Spirit creatively communicated His love to a group of faithful, battle-weary saints.

So how might we know if the Spirit wants to speak to us in this way? Just pay attention. Be attentive to any image or picture that comes to mind as you quiet yourself before the Lord. Don't dismiss it simply because the image initially seems fleeting or irrelevant. Take a moment and reflect upon it. See if the image becomes clearer or perhaps the meaning becomes evident.

Dreams

One other biblical category of seeing is dreams. Throughout the Bible, God often spoke to people through dreams. Jacob, Joseph (in the Old and New Testament), Pharaoh, Daniel, the Magi, the wife of Pontius Pilate are a few examples. Peter's words in Acts 2:17 that "Your old men will dream dreams ..." indicate that God continues to speak in this way. My friend, Tom Doyle, has written a book chronicling numerous examples of Muslims coming to Christ as a result of seeing Jesus in a dream[2].

I recently attended a psychic fair as part of a team of Christians offering dream interpretation for anyone interested. While clearly being outside of my comfort zone, I was amazed at how God consistently communicated a message to people in their dreams. Unfortunately we often dismiss our dreams as being unimportant, due to how weird or confusing they might be. But what if we believed that God may be speaking to us through them?

In order to grow in this, begin paying attention to dreams that seem vivid, significant or are recurring. Write the dream down so you don't forget it. Then prayerfully ask for the Spirit's help to discern what God may be saying. In Genesis 41, when Pharaoh asked Joseph to interpret his dream, Joseph wisely responded, "I cannot do it ... but God will give Pharaoh the answer he desires" (verse 16). We need the Spirit to help us.

From a biblical perspective, the key to hearing God speak through a dream is in understanding the symbolism in it. Sometimes we err in assuming a symbol is literal. Recently a friend asked my wife and me to help her discern the meaning of a dream. In it, she was in a large airport. Now we might assume this means that travel is in her future, but what if the airport is symbolic? What do people do in airports? They wait. As we prayed about the meaning, we felt that part of this dream was describing a significant season of waiting our friend is experiencing.

Also helpful to remember is that context is crucial. The color green in a dream may symbolize life, but it could also symbolize envy. Prayerfully understanding the context can help determine what a symbol might mean. Clearly, dreams and visions are biblical ways in which God's Spirit may speak to us. Are we open to that possibility?

Sensing

A fourth way the Spirit may speak is through sensing. Whereas hearing focuses on words and seeing focuses on images, sensing focuses on what we sense in our spirit, our body, or our emotions. For example, in Luke 5, Jesus healed a man and declared that his sins were forgiven. Cool miracle, right? Not if you were a Pharisee. "The Pharisees and the teachers of the law began thinking to themselves, 'Who is this fellow who speaks blasphemy? Who can forgive sins but God alone?' *Jesus knew what they were thinking*" (verses 21–22, italics added).

This kind of sensing may initially appear as little more than a gut feeling or an intuition. But if it begins to gain traction in your spirit, pay attention.

Our Spirit

Jesus knew what they were thinking. Some people call this a "word of knowledge." I realize that this term is often loaded with negative baggage, but let's not throw out the baby with the bathwater. After all, in Ephesians 1:17 Paul refers to the Spirit as "the Spirit of wisdom and revelation." The Spirit may reveal to us things we would not know otherwise.

I recently read a pastor's description of an occasion when a woman approached him for prayer after a worship service. Before she began speaking, he knew in his spirit that she was tremendously afraid of becoming an alcoholic. Further conversation revealed this to be the case.[3]

God once revealed to a friend of mine in prayer that the man she was dating was also dating someone else. When they met again, she asked him and he hesitantly admitted the truth. Who knows how long he would have waited. In revealing this to her, God protected her heart from further pain. This kind of sensing may initially appear as little more than a gut feeling or an intuition. But if it begins to gain traction in your spirit, pay attention.

Our Body

Another way we may experience this sensing dimension of the Spirit's ministry is in our physical bodies. In Luke 8, a woman touched Jesus' garment and was immediately healed. Jesus stopped and said, "Someone touched me; I know that power has gone out from me" (Luke 8:46). He sensed something in His physical body.

A friend of mine was in a grocery store one day and began to experience pain in his shoulder. He sensed the Spirit was using his pain to communicate something about a gentleman standing nearby. He hesitantly approached the man.

"I know this is a bit weird to ask, but are you experiencing shoulder pain?"

The man nearly jumped out of his skin. "I am. I've had chronic shoulder pain for months. Why do you ask?"

"I sometimes sense things in my body as a way that God communicates to me," my friend said. "My shoulder began hurting the moment I walked into this store. Would you mind if I prayed for you?"

"Of course not," the man replied. "Go for it."

So my friend prayed for this man and God healed him. How cool is that? I know that's a fairly dramatic example, but it does highlight how the Spirit may want to speak to us using our physical bodies. Are we paying attention to that?

Our Emotions

In addition to speaking to us through our physical bodies, the Spirit may also communicate through our emotions. As we pray for someone, we may experience a sense of anxiety, despair, or depression. God may be revealing how to pray for this person as we feel what they feel. Earlier I mentioned my bubble wrap experience with the group of missionaries. As that picture came to mind, I was immediately filled with a sense of compassion for them and began to weep. God gave me a small taste of His heart for these dear people.

Messengers

A fifth way the Spirit may speak to us is through messengers—a teaching we hear from our pastor, a magazine article or book we read, a conversation with a trusted friend. In Galatians 2, Paul was God's messenger to Peter, confronting him with the truth that he was not living according to the gospel. Part of what characterizes biblical community is speaking the truth to one another in love (see Ephesians 4:15). Often God uses these relationships to speak to our hearts.

One morning while exercising, I watched a short segment of a well-known Bible teacher on TV. This person quoted an unfamiliar passage from Isaiah. While I found the Scripture interesting, it didn't connect with anything in my life. Later that day, as I prayed with a woman experiencing difficulty with one of her children, the Isaiah passage from that morning came to mind. Her heart felt encouraged when I shared the passage with her. God used a messenger on television to communicate with me so that I could be a messenger of His truth to someone in need.

In the Bible, these messengers sometimes come in the form of an angel. I know this is way outside the box, but it is biblical. Examples include Abraham, Joshua, Gideon, Mary, the shepherds in Luke 2, and Peter, to name a few.

When my wife was pregnant with one of our children, a good friend of ours came over one evening. He seemed a bit shook up. Concerned, we asked if everything was okay. He hesitantly shared about an angel that appeared to him that morning with a message regarding our soon-to-be-born child. We were definitely paying attention! Over the years, that angelic message has guided our prayers for that child.

While I'm not aware that I have ever encountered an angel, Scripture encourages us to be open to the possibility. In Hebrews 13:2 we read, "Do not forget to show hospitality to strangers, for by so doing some people have shown hospitality to angels without knowing it."

Isn't it fun to realize all the varying ways the Spirit may want to communicate with us? He longs to help us hear His voice. After all, we have a love relationship with Him. He *wants* to help us grow in this. Our job is to be spiritually attentive to what we hear, see, or sense. Who knows what doors may open, what ministry may happen, what wisdom may be given as we tune into the Spirit's voice?

HOLY SPIRIT LABORATORY

Think for a few moments about specific ways the Spirit has spoken to you in the past. How open are you to hearing Him speak in other ways? Take a moment and ask the Spirit to expand your experience of hearing His voice.

How Do We Know It's God?

Without a doubt the biggest question that arises whenever this subject is discussed is this: *How do I know if it is God speaking? Maybe it's the pizza I had for dinner.* With something so subjective and mystical, how can we recognize the voice of the Spirit? That's a great question that needs to be addressed. But before we go there, I want to point out that sometimes we let these questions stir up so much fear in our hearts that we dismiss the possibility of hearing God speak. In fact, I find that many Christians have more faith in the devil's ability to deceive than they do in God's ability to speak. This is truly unfortunate. We need to remember that God longs to speak to His children and has given us His Spirit to help us hear.

Many Christians have more faith in the devil's ability to deceive than they do in God's ability to speak.

So how can we know whether or not God is speaking to us? How can we know whether or not the picture in our head or the thought that comes to mind is from the Spirit? Let me offer four simple tests when trying to discern whether or not God is speaking:

1. The Scripture Test

Our ultimate authority is God's Word. We need to measure every thought, word, and deed by that standard. In light of that, a critical question to ask when discerning whether or not God is speaking is this: *Does this violate any principle or teaching in Scripture?* If someone is listening to God and hears in their spirit, *You are a loser. God doesn't love you. You have made too many mistakes for Him to ever forgive*, that person can immediately discern this is not from God. God's Word clearly communicates the wonder of the gospel — that in Christ, we are loved and forgiven forever. So the Bible is a critical filter for us as we listen to God's voice. (We'll talk more about this in Chapter 12.)

2. The Tone Test

Whenever we listen in prayer and a word or thought comes to mind, it's important to ask, *how* is this word or picture being communicated to me? Does it feel forceful and hurried? Does it feel condemning or perhaps confusing? As we saw in the last chapter with the example of Elijah, God doesn't bully us, but instead speaks in a gentle, loving way. He can still be direct and communicate challenging truths, but the tone of the message will feel gentle and loving. So pay attention to the tone of what is being communicated. Is it consistent with what we know of God's character — His grace, His love, His compassion?

3. The Resonance Test

Any time we sense the Lord may be speaking, it's helpful to ask ourselves, *Does this resonate in my spirit?* I mentioned earlier that when I see a fleeting or vague picture in my mind as I pray, I try to wait a few moments to see if the picture gains clarity. Sometimes it fades away, but other times when I wait, the picture becomes more vivid. It begins to carry more weight in my spirit. When that happens, I pay attention.

One often overlooked facet of this resonance test is found in community. We need our brothers and sisters in Christ to help us discern God's voice. When you sense the Lord saying something to you, don't hesitate to ask a few people you trust to pray with you about this. See if they confirm what you are sensing.

4. The Fruit Test

In Matthew 7, Jesus urges us to discern the ministry of false prophets by using the fruit test—"By their fruit you will recognize them" (Matthew 7:20). We can discern whether or not something comes from God by observing the fruit of the person's life and words. Similarly, we can discern the voice of the Spirit by evaluating the fruit over time. Do we see evidence that what we heard is actually bearing fruit?

For instance, perhaps as you pray for someone, you see in your mind a picture that you share with them. Weeks later they tell you how meaningful that picture has been in their walk with Christ. That's fruit ... and it's incredibly encouraging. Over time, we begin to better discern what is from God and what isn't from God, simply by evaluating the results. Paul describes exactly what fruit the Spirit's voice might result in: "love, joy, peace, patience, kindness, goodness, faithfulness, gentleness, and self-control" (Galatians 5:22–23 NIV84). If our hearing results in more of this occurring, we know we are on the right track.

Don't let fear keep you from the wonderful adventure of listening to the Spirit's voice. He wants to communicate with you. Ask Him to do so and then start paying attention. Who knows what might result from that simple decision.

Chapter Six

Hearing the Spirit for Others

—〰—

Several months ago, I met with a pastor friend to reconnect. We hadn't seen each other for a few months and wanted to catch up. As we began the conversation, Dick mentioned that he had been praying for me earlier that day and had asked the Lord if He wanted him to share anything with me. Immediately, a Scripture passage came to his mind—the story in Matthew 17 where Jesus tells Peter to go catch a fish and find in the fish's mouth the coin needed to pay taxes. What Dick heard in his spirit were these words: *The Lord hears your cry. There is an answer to your financial situation. I have the answer. It's about to be caught.* So as we met that day, he shared that message with me.

What Dick had no way of knowing was that we were indeed in the midst of a very financially challenging season as a church. I felt that God had given our church a vision to expand our influence, and yet I found myself disheartened at being so far behind budget. My friend's words encouraged me to persevere and trust God in this frustrating season. Four months later, our church experienced an incredible financial turnaround. The Lord did indeed have the answer and we were about to "catch" it.

This story provides a vivid reminder to me of the power of hearing the Spirit for other people. Dick's attentiveness to the Spirit on my behalf greatly encouraged me in that season. Had he not asked the Lord that question about me, we would have met and visited about our ministries, including our church's financial situation. Dick may have reminded me of God's provision in Matthew 17 — but it wouldn't have made the same impact. How amazing to realize that before I mentioned anything to my friend, God was already aware of my situation and was actively at work.

It's Okay to Use the P-Word

I could tell dozens and dozens more stories like that — of God giving someone a specific word or Scripture for another person. When that word was shared with them, they felt wonderfully encouraged. The Bible uses a specific word to describe this ministry of the Spirit. While this word at times results in a knee-jerk, negative reaction from some Christ followers, I hope you will give it fresh consideration. The word is "prophecy."

For many Christians, the word prophecy brings to mind various end times predictions and certain Bible teachers who focus on the book of Revelation. This "foretelling the future" is certainly one way the word is used in Scripture. Many Old Testament prophecies accurately predict specific details about the birth and life of Jesus.

That, however, is not the only way the word "prophecy" is used in the Bible. Many Scriptures use the word to describe what I experienced with my friend — God bringing something to a person's mind that when shared with others results in spiritual fruit. For instance, in 1 Corinthians 14 we read this description of prophecy:

> Follow the way of love and eagerly desire spiritual gifts, especially prophecy ... The one who prophesies speaks to people for their strengthening, encouraging and comfort. Anyone who speaks in a tongue edifies themselves, but the one who prophesies edifies the church .... Two or three prophets should speak, and the others should weigh carefully what is said. And if a revelation comes to someone who is sitting down, the first speaker should stop. For you can all prophecy in turn so that everyone may be instructed and encouraged.
>
> 1 Corinthians 14:1, 3–4, 29–31

From these verses, we learn several practical truths about prophecy. First, prophecy is not something *we* conjure up but rather comes *from* the Spirit. The Spirit initiates the prophetic. In addition, we learn that prophecy *spontaneously* comes to someone's mind. Paul uses the word "revelation" in verse 30 to describe how someone receives a prophecy. God spontaneously reveals it to them.

We also learn from this passage the purpose of prophecy. The Spirit gives it to strengthen (or build up), encourage and comfort other believers. My friend Dick's prophetic words to me that day encouraged my heart, giving me strength to persevere. Paul clearly asserts that prophecy—when functioning properly—can be an incredible blessing to one another in the body of Christ.

So here's how we might define prophecy[1]:

Prophecy is the communication of something God spontaneously brings to our awareness, resulting in a person being strengthened, encouraged, or comforted.

Notice the two parts of this definition. Prophecy first of all involves God bringing to our awareness something we did not know or perceive by natural means. In the previous two chapters, we discussed how God may speak to us in this way.

Secondly, prophecy involves the *communication* of that thought or perception to others. Had my friend Dick kept to himself what he had heard in prayer, this would not have been a prophetic word—and we both would have missed a huge blessing. God intends that prophecy be a blessing to the body of Christ. It doesn't have to be kooky or weird. What a great privilege to hear from God for someone else, and then share it with them, bringing encouragement and comfort.

What a great privilege to hear from God for someone else, and then share it with them, bringing encouragement and comfort.

Are Old and New Testament Prophecy the Same?

So if prophecy is as beneficial as just described, why don't we practice this more often? Why isn't this ministry of the Spirit more frequently experienced in churches? Here's the biggest reason: We assume that New Testament prophecy is the same as Old Testament prophecy. And that scares us. In the Old Testament, a prophet spoke the very words of God. Their words had absolute, divine authority. So they could say, "Thus says the Lord," and mean it. Notice how God describes the prophet's ministry in Deuteronomy 18:18–20:

> I will raise up for them a prophet like you from among their fellow Israelites, and I will put my words in his mouth. He will tell them everything I command him. I myself will call to account anyone who does not listen to my words that the prophet speaks in my name. But a prophet who presumes to speak in my name anything I have not commanded, or a prophet who speaks in the name of other gods, is to be put to death.

This is serious stuff. A legitimate prophet of the Lord was bestowed with divine authority to speak the very words of God. If people didn't obey the words of an Old Testament prophet, they were held accountable for disobeying God. Some of the words of God's prophets became Old Testament Scripture and were given divine authority.

In the New Testament, people also wrote and spoke God's words—but they were not called prophets. They were called apostles. In 2 Peter 3:2, we read, "I want you to recall the words spoken in the past by the holy prophets and the command given by our Lord and Savior through your apostles." New Testament apostles (like Paul, Peter, and John) were, in a sense, the counterparts to the Old Testament prophets. But prophecy still plays a role in the New Testament.

Prophecy in the New Testament ... is not a "Thus says the Lord" kind of pronouncement. Rather, it may or may not be from God, and thus needs to be tested and weighed.

We already read Paul's words in 1 Corinthians 14 about prophecy being utilized and encouraged in the church, but this prophecy significantly differs from Old Testament prophecy. Look again at what Paul says in verse 29, "Two or three prophets should speak, and the others should weigh carefully what is said." Interesting. He encourages them to *weigh carefully* what is said; in other words, test and weigh what is spoken to determine what is and isn't from God.

Clearly, prophecy in the New Testament no longer carries the weight of divine authority. It is not a "Thus says the Lord" kind of pronouncement. Rather, it may or may not be from God, and thus needs to be tested and weighed. Paul reiterates this in 1 Thessalonians 5:20–21, "Do not treat prophecies with contempt, but test them all; hold on to what is good." Again ... test and weigh.

When correctly utilized, prophecy encourages, strengthens, and comforts people in the body of Christ.

I find it troubling that many Christians completely dismiss Paul's clear command in this verse: "Do not treat prophecies with contempt." We ignore or dismiss this kind of listening to the Spirit; usually because of abuses we have seen in the past where people express it with an Old Testament authority.

A friend of mine grew up in a church where prophecy was spoken with a "Thus says the Lord" kind of authority, often focused on pointing out people's sins. No wonder some people run for cover when the word "prophecy" is mentioned. But it doesn't need to be that way. As Paul describes in 1 Corinthians 14:3, "But the one who prophesies speaks to people for their strengthening, encouraging and comfort." When correctly utilized, prophecy encourages, strengthens, and comforts people in the body of Christ. It's a really good thing!

Here Are a Few Clarifying Questions Regarding Prophecy

In order to grow in the ministry of prophecy, we need to address a few important questions.

Are teaching and prophecy the same?

While both prophecy and teaching involve communicating truth to the body that can bring encouragement, strength, and comfort, they are fundamentally different. Teaching involves the deliberate study of the Bible and the communication of those truths in a way that people can apply to their lives. With prophecy, however, God *spontaneously* brings to our awareness something He wants us to communicate. In 1 Corinthians 14:29-31, Paul describes a situation where multiple people receive spontaneous prophecies (revelation). As we discussed in the previous chapter, these may come in the form of a picture, a phrase, a Scripture, or just a sense — but when shared, they often result in wonderful impact.

A friend received an email from an acquaintance in another state who was considering planting a church. My friend did not know this person or their situation well but felt prompted to pray about it. As he prayed, the words "Lucas" and "Downs" kept coming to his mind. He then began to sense in his spirit the Lord saying, *"They need to represent me to Lucas and Downs."* He also saw a picture of a house with the number 181 on it. Not knowing what

All of us can grow in our experience of prophecy — regardless of whether or not we have this gift.

any of this meant, he called the couple and told them what he had seen. They excitedly shared with him that Lucas and Downs were the two towns near them where they had been thinking of planting a church. They also explained that 181 was the number of the highway that connected the towns! Needless to say, those words brought incredible encouragement to their hearts, reminding them that God knew their situation.

Can every Christian experience prophecy?

Absolutely! Remember Peter's words in Acts 2:17-18 on the day of Pentecost: "Your sons and daughters will prophesy, your young men will see visions, your old men will dream dreams. *Even on my servants, both men and women, I will pour out my Spirit ... and they will prophesy"* (italics added). God clearly declares that one of the defining characteristics of the Spirit's ministry in the church will be a widespread experience of prophecy—on young and old, men and women; even servants will get in on the action. God longs to speak to and through His children, bringing encouragement to His church.

Now certain people in the body of Christ will function more effectively in this. They have what the New Testament refers to as the spiritual gift of prophecy (1 Corinthians 12:10, 13:2). However, just because some have a particular gift in this doesn't mean the rest of the body can't enjoy the experience as well. Even though some have a gift of evangelism, God calls us all to share Christ with others. Even though some have a spiritual gift of mercy, God urges us all to be merciful. People with a spiritual gift in a specific area simply function at a higher capacity in that area than the rest of us. This means that all of us can grow in our experience of prophecy—regardless of whether or not we have this gift. Having seen first-hand how life-changing this can be in people's lives, I often pray that God will increase my ability to encourage and comfort others in this way. How about you?

HOLY SPIRIT LABORATORY

Paul specifically encourages us to seek a deeper experience of prophecy. "Follow the way of love and eagerly desire gifts of the Spirit, especially prophecy" (1 Corinthians 14:1). *Eagerly desire this.*

Is prophecy something you eagerly desire? Why or why not? Take a few minutes to pray about your answer to this question. Do you have any fears or concerns? Do you long to grow in this?

Ask God to increase your ability to hear Him in this way.

How do I test a prophetic word?

As we saw earlier in 1 Thessalonians 5:20-21 and 1 Corinthians 14:29, Paul reminds us that we shouldn't assume a prophetic word is from God, no matter who shares it with us. Rather, he urges us to test any prophetic word that is given to us. So how exactly do we do that? In chapter five, I mentioned four simple tests to use when discerning whether or not something we hear is from God. Those same tests apply in this situation as well.

The Scripture Test: Does this prophetic word violate any principle or teaching in the Bible?

The Tone Test: Does the tone of this prophecy reflect the heart and character of God? Is it loving, gentle, without condemnation — reflecting God's heart? Or is it forceful, guilt-filled, condemning — reflecting our enemy's voice?

The Resonance Test: Does this prophecy resonate in your spirit? Does it resonate with people who know you well?

The Fruit Test: Does this prophecy bear fruit in our lives? Does it bring encouragement, strength, comfort? Does it accurately speak to an area God wants to focus on?

Whatever is from God, we embrace. Whatever is not, we let go. Plenty of times, people have given me a prophetic word that didn't resonate with me in the least. Even after thinking and praying about it for a few days, I still felt no weight or connection to what the person shared. That's okay. In that case, I'm free to determine that it wasn't from God. That conclusion says nothing about the gifting or character of the person who gave this word to me. Rather, it reminds us that none of us hear from God perfectly. As Paul says in 1 Corinthians 13, "now we see in a mirror dimly" (verse 12, NASB). We will not have 100 percent clarity until we get to heaven, which is why we always need to test any prophetic word.

A Less Threatening Phrase Can Calm People's Fears

I realize that some Christian leaders may hesitate to encourage the practice of prophecy in their church because of the negative baggage associated with this word. The moment we use the word "prophecy" at church, we fear being labeled or misunderstood by others. I totally understand — which is why at our church, we often use a different term to refer to this kind of praying, in order to minimize any weirdness. We call it "listening prayer."

We have "listening prayer teams" that pray for others in this way. In listening prayer, we tune in to God as we pray for someone and then communicate what we hear. That's prophecy—but we don't need to use that specific word to describe it, especially if that word may create a barrier of fear or suspicion. All we're doing is listening to God as we pray for someone. Amazing ministry can happen when we make room for God to speak in this way.

Whatever is from God, we embrace. Whatever is not, we let go.

So once we are convinced that God does indeed want to communicate in this way and that biblical safeguards are in place to test whatever is shared, how do we go about practicing this with other people? That's the topic for the next chapter.

Chapter Seven

How to Share a Prophetic Word ... Without Being Weird

—⟋⟋⟍—

M any of us have likely heard the prophecy horror stories ... maybe we've even experienced them ourselves. Someone "has a word" for us, and yet after this "word" is given, we feel more beaten up or confused than encouraged. No wonder we hesitate to give much credence to this ministry. The forceful, direct, "thus says the Lord" type of prophetic words tend to do more harm than good. But does that mean that God wasn't speaking? What if God *was* actually speaking, but the *means* of delivering the message got in the way?

I am convinced that many Christians want nothing to do with prophecy simply because of how they have seen prophetic words communicated. Wouldn't it be awesome if there was a way to give a prophetic word to a person without all the forcefulness and weirdness? Actually there is. In this chapter, I'd like to teach you how to do just that. At our church, we often use the term "release" to describe the sharing of a prophetic word. So let's talk about how we can release a word to someone without causing offense. An effective release contains two essential elements.

That Crazy Little Thing Called Love

Look carefully at Paul's words in 1 Corinthians 13:1-2.

> If I speak in the tongues of men or of angels, but do not have love, I am only a resounding gong or a clanging cymbal. If I have the gift of prophecy and can fathom all mysteries and all knowledge, and if I have a faith that can move mountains, but do not have love, I am nothing.

Paul encourages us to imagine a person with the strongest prophetic gift possible, fathoming mysteries and receiving amazingly accurate insights and visions for people. All pretty impressive, right? Not if they don't have love. Paul says that if a person has a gift of prophecy that is off the charts but doesn't have love, they are nothing. Absolutely nothing.

Without love, any prophetic ministry is meaningless.

Without love, any prophetic ministry is meaningless. Whenever we pray for someone, love should be our ultimate motivation. This means expressing genuine care and concern, being attentive to them. After all, this is a real person, a person whom God loves dearly. We have the privilege of expressing that love in *how* we pray for them.

Later in 1 Corinthians 13, Paul tells us that "Love is patient, love is kind ... It does not dishonor others, it is not self-seeking ... It always protects, always trusts, always hopes, always perseveres" (1 Corinthians 13:4, 5, 7). This description should characterize the prophetic ministry. When we release prophetic words in a forceful manner ("You should do this and this") or in an authoritative way ("God told me you need to ..."), we have already violated the principle of love. We are not honoring the person or trusting them; we are being self-seeking and rude. Remember, our ultimate objective is not simply to hear from God for this person but to love them. No matter what happens in prayer, we want to make sure this person feels cared for by us.

Love becomes extremely important in the event we hear something negative as we pray for someone. For instance, maybe as we pray we sense that this person's marriage is struggling, or perhaps we see a cloud of discouragement hanging over them. What do we do in these instances?

First, we must examine our own heart and make sure we are not harboring anything negative against this person. Once that's done, we then have a few options, depending on our relationship with this person. If we don't know them, we can simply pray into the positive side of this. For example, if you sense a marriage is struggling, pray for God's blessing upon the marriage. If you sense anger is an issue, pray for grace and patience.

However, if we have a personal relationship with them and feel that the Lord want us to share the information, we can do so, but always in a loving and compassionate manner. When praying on a prayer team for someone, you may want to wait for a one-on-one opportunity with the person before you share. In general, it is wise to avoid a rebuke or correction. Pray for God to give you wisdom in the event that the prophetic word you receive is negative.

Humility Is Essential

In addition to love, a second essential element in releasing a prophetic word is humility. When a person begins ministering in the prophetic, pride can be a very enticing temptation. That first time you hear God speak to you about a person's situation—something you had no prior knowledge of—can be a rush. How awesome to realize that God spoke to you! Often the person receiving the prayer expresses awe at how powerful the prayer time was. Quite honestly, this kind of stuff can easily go to our head. We start to feel a bit proud of our ability to hear God speak. But of course, pride is the antithesis of God's heart. "God opposes the proud but shows favor to the humble" (1 Peter 5:5).

Pastor and author Jack Deere writes:

> Humility is one of the main character qualities of all the great prophets [Moses, John the Baptist, Jeremiah]. Humility is the pathway to friendship with God. It is very simple: God deals with the proud at a distance, but with the humble it's up close and personal.[1]

When pride begins to infiltrate the heart of someone operating in the realm of prophecy, disaster can result. We become forceful in how we communicate a prophetic word or we get offended when someone doesn't receive the word we spoke. We compare ourselves to others, feeling jealous of those with a greater prophetic capacity or feeling superior to those with lesser ability. We easily forget that our capacity to hear God's Spirit ultimately comes from God Himself. We can't make this happen or manufacture it.

When releasing a word to someone, humility is absolutely essential. What does that look like? Here's a basic and essential principle: *Be tentative in how you communicate anything you sense God saying.* In other words, a prophetic word should be offered as a *possibility* for others to consider, to weigh, to test, to discern if it truly is from God. Rather than saying *"God told me"* or *"The Lord says,"* say something like, *"This is what I think I'm hearing ..."* or *"I believe God might be saying..."* We should not make declarations from on high that God has spoken. After all, we are not certain that He has. All we are doing is offering what we think God is saying, which then gives the hearer the freedom and opportunity to test for themselves whether or not this is from God.

This totally takes the pressure off. When I first waded into the waters of listening to God on behalf of someone else, I was initially afraid of hearing nothing or of saying something that didn't resonate at all with the other person. It terrified me, so much so that I hesitated to say anything. How incredibly freeing it was when I realized

> *Be tentative in how you communicate anything you sense God saying.*

that the pressure is not on me to release a perfectly accurate word. My responsibility is to humbly and lovingly share what I think I'm hearing. That's it. The person receiving the prophetic prayer is responsible to test and weigh it, rejecting what isn't from God and embracing what is.

Here's a Simple Model for Listening and Releasing

So how can we make this prophetic experience a more normal part of praying for other people? Let me share a simple model you can use anytime you pray prophetically for someone[2].

Step One: Be Attentive to the Spirit

Begin by quieting your heart as you start to pray for someone. Don't feel the need to fill the prayer time with words. It's important to be still and listen. If you are concerned that the silence may feel awkward, simply let the person know that you intend to be still for a few moments in order to quiet your heart before the Lord.

Quietly ask the Lord to speak to you, and then be attentive to any words, pictures, phrases, Scripture references, or sensations that come to your awareness. As specific things arise, wait to see if they gain traction in your soul. Sometimes thoughts are simply fleeting thoughts that dissipate in seconds. Other times, an initial thought will stay with you and gain traction. Pay attention to those thoughts.

At times you may find it helpful to ask the Lord a question as you are praying. My wife often quietly asks the Lord, *How do You see this person's heart?* It is amazing the ways God answers that question, giving Raylene insights into what pleases God about this person.

Step Two: Tell the person what you are hearing, seeing, or sensing.

Once a thought or picture or phrase gains some traction in your spirit, take a moment and share with this person what you are hearing, seeing or sensing. For instance, "As we have been praying, I keep hearing the words 'Be bold'" Or "I keep seeing this picture of _____." If a Scripture reference comes to mind, share the passage with them.

Step Three: If you sense the meaning of what you are hearing, tell them that as well.

Sometimes as you see a particular image or hear a particular word, God may give you insight into what it means. Feel free to share this with the person, but do so tentatively, as we described earlier. You may be wrong in your interpretation, but you might be right as well. Remember it is *their* responsibility to test it.

The other day as I prayed for a pastor, I saw in my spirit a wheelbarrow with a flower in it. This pastor was pushing the wheelbarrow. As I explained the picture to him, I felt that I knew what it meant—that God saw this man's faithfulness in ministry and was pleased. So I shared this with him.

As we continued praying, the image again came to mind, only this time I saw multiple handles on the wheelbarrow. Immediately I felt that God wanted to encourage this person to delegate some of his ministry responsibilities. So I again shared my thoughts with him.

Step Four: Pray into what you have seen or heard.

Once you share the word or picture and its meaning—if you have a sense of it—you can then "pray into" what you have seen. In the wheelbarrow example, after sharing what I saw and what I thought it meant, I then prayed into it. *"Lord, thank You that You see Mark's faithfulness and You are pleased with him. Father I pray that Mark would be able to delegate tasks and responsibilities so that his load is lightened. Bring the people he needs for that to happen and give him wisdom in choosing those people."*

> *We're not just interested in transferring information. We want God to move in this person's life.*

This prayer piece is an important part of an effective release. We're not just interested in transferring information. We want God to move in this person's life. When someone shares a prophetic word and then neglects to specifically pray into that, they miss an opportunity to more fully release God's activity in the person's life.

Wade in!

So there you have it—a simple way to begin wading into listening prayer (or prophecy). It's not complicated, nor does it need to be weird or heavy. Any of us can experience this as we pray for another person, opening up wonderful doors for the Spirit to encourage and comfort. Which raises an obvious question: *Why then don't we do this more often?* If we believe the New Testament teaches that God wants prophecy to regularly function in the body of Christ, what keeps us from engaging in this more frequently?

The obvious answer to that question is fear. To pray in this way scares us. What if God doesn't say anything and we end up looking foolish? This can actually be a healthy fear, because it keeps us humble, reminding us that apart from God's Spirit, we can do nothing. For this reason, I try to pray in a team whenever possible. Multiple people listening in prayer helps lessen the sense of pressure we feel to always hear the Spirit.

We may also fear being wrong and sharing something that doesn't resonate in the least with the person. That certainly can happen—in fact, it *will* happen. Plan on it. None of us hear perfectly. But remember our ultimate motivation for growing in the prophetic—love. A genuine love for the person. The Bible tells us that perfect love casts out fear (1 John 4:18). Granted it may feel risky to share what we sense the Lord saying, but think of the alternative. What if God wanted to use you to impart blessing but your fear kept you from saying anything?

Love moves us to take the risk and humbly share what we think God is saying.

Love moves us to take the risk and humbly share what we think God is saying. If it doesn't come from

God, it won't resonate with the person and they will simply ignore it. No harm done. If it comes from God, it can be a source of encouragement, strength, or comfort. That to me is worth the risk. Having frequently received prophetic prayer from others, I know firsthand the blessing it can be. I'm glad those praying for me were willing to take the risk.

Several months ago, a friend of mine shared with me that he and his wife were struggling in their marriage. We discussed some of the challenges and transitions they had been experiencing. As we parted, I promised him I would pray for them. The next morning in my time with the Lord, I began to pray for my friend. However, instead of doing all the talking, I decided to wait and listen for God to share anything with me. Suddenly, a picture of a bulldozer came to mind, out of the blue. I didn't know what this meant but it seemed significant.

When I finished praying, I emailed my friend and told him what I saw in prayer. "Couldn't it have been something more like a gazelle?" he jokingly asked. He agreed to pray about it.

He called me a few days later with an amazing story.

"Alan, you'll never believe this. You know how you emailed me about a bulldozer the other day?"

"Yeah," I replied.

"Initially I dismissed it as being one of your weird prayer things. But then yesterday, my wife and I were talking about our marriage—and out of the blue, she said, 'I feel like you have been a bulldozer in how you have treated me. You haven't really listened to my opinions about decisions. You've just done what you wanted to do.'"

Needless to say, he was floored. Her using that same bulldozer imagery caused a major awakening in his soul. He finally heard what she was saying and, instead of ignoring it, embraced it as true. He had been selfish, controlling, proud — and in the process had alienated and hurt his wife. I talked with him recently and he once again referred to that bulldozer prophecy as a major turning point in their marriage, a moment in which God opened my friend's eyes to see something he had ignored. Life has now been poured into that relationship.

When I think about experiences like that, I'm reminded of the profound impact that prophecy can make in people's lives. No wonder Paul urges us in 1 Corinthians 14:1 to "eagerly desire ... prophecy." It really can be a huge blessing in the body of Christ.

Prophecy in the Church

Before we finish this chapter, I'd like to make a few comments to pastors regarding how prophecy might function in the local church. Your church doesn't need to be a charismatic church in order to enjoy the blessings of this ministry. Here are some simple practices our church observes to encourage prophecy without raising unnecessary concerns:

- Because the word "prophecy" often carries a lot of negative baggage for people, don't feel like you must use that specific word. Simply encourage them to listen to God as they pray for others.
- Invite those with a desire to pray for others to some training where you begin teaching them how to listen to God and how they might release a word to someone else. Make sure the training involves opportunities to practice this with each other.
- Identify those people who seem to have some proficiency in this kind of prayer and

begin building a prayer team that practices this. Have these teams available to pray for people after worship services.

• Be attentive during worship services to the Spirit speaking, giving you a word or picture for the congregation. When that happens to me, I will sometimes share it at the end of worship. I release it the same way described earlier in this chapter. Not, "God told me," but rather, "During that last worship song, a picture came to my mind that I believe the Lord may be giving us this morning." I describe the picture and then pray into what I think the meaning is.

By modeling this to the congregation, others will feel the freedom to hear the Lord in this way and learn how to gently release a word without causing offense.

So what are you waiting for? Ask the Spirit to help you grow in this area ... and then wade in!

HOLY SPIRIT LABORATORY

The next time you pray for someone, take time to listen to God on their behalf. See if the Lord brings to mind a picture, a word, a Scripture. If that happens, wait a few moments to see if it gains traction or to see if you sense the meaning of it. Then release it to the person in a loving, humble way. Pray into that as well.

Afterwards, ask the person how the experience was for them. How did they feel? Did it resonate with them?

Section Three

Experiencing the Spirit in Healing and Prayer

—⁊⁊⁊—

Chapter Eight

The Spirit of Healing

—⚏—

One morning, I woke up feeling awful. Nauseated, achy, feverish … not good. Having planned on attending a conference with my staff that day, I immediately called and told them I wouldn't be coming. Then I laid back down to rest, desperately hoping I wouldn't have to throw up (I prefer a root canal to vomiting). When Raylene heard that I was sick, she laid her hands on me and asked God to heal my body. Within minutes, the nausea and fever were gone. I got up, showered, and headed to the conference, missing only a small portion of it.

The ministry of healing can be a normal part of our experience as Christians. Rather than the showy, forceful, or manipulative approaches we see at times on television, healing prayer can be a wonderfully refreshing way in which we experience the Spirit at work in our ordinary lives.

Why Does Jesus Heal?

We can learn much about healing by looking at the life of Jesus. When Jesus began His ministry, He walked into a synagogue in His home town and read a passage of Scripture which He immediately declared to be His job description:

> The Spirit of the Lord is on me, because he has anointed me to proclaim good news to the poor. He has sent me to proclaim freedom for the prisoners and recovery of sight for the blind, to set the oppressed free, to proclaim the year of the Lord's favor.   Luke 4:18-19

Jesus declared that healing would be a key facet of His ministry in the Spirit. Immediately after this, Luke described multiple examples of Jesus doing this very thing (see Luke 4:38-41, 5:12-25). So why was healing such a critically important part of Jesus' ministry?

One, these healings provided dramatic demonstrations of God's power, boldly declaring Jesus' supernatural authority and thus confirming His divinity and teaching. The ministry of healing visibly demonstrated that the kingdom of God had come in power, driving back the works of the enemy (see Luke 11:14-23).

But there's another reason as well. Jesus' ministry of healing demonstrated His compassionate heart. In Luke 5, Jesus was approached by a man afflicted with leprosy, a highly contagious disease causing physical disfigurement as well as societal ostracism. People avoided this unclean person at all costs. Imagine the emotional, physical, and social trauma this man experienced every moment of his life. Complete rejection and utter isolation. He said to Jesus, "Lord if you are willing, you can make me clean."

Jesus' ministry of healing demonstrated His compassionate heart.

Jesus' reaction communicates volumes. "Jesus reached out his hand and touched the man. 'I am willing,' he said. 'Be clean!' And immediately the leprosy left him" (verse 13). Notice His first response: He *touched* the man, a man who hadn't been touched in years. Then Jesus spoke three powerful words: "I am willing." Jesus' compassion moved Him to heal. Even when Jesus felt

> *Healing prayer enables us to demonstrate the compassion of Jesus toward those who are suffering.*

tired and needed time alone, His compassion moved Him to heal the sick that came to Him (see Matthew 14:13–14).

This is God's heart toward sickness. God's original creation had no sickness, nor will there be any in heaven. Sickness is a result of a fallen world infected by sin. No wonder Jesus healed when He saw people suffering from various illnesses. God's ultimate purpose and plan involve reversing the effects of this fallen world, including its sicknesses and disease. His heart is a heart of compassion toward the sick and suffering.

I realize this raises all sorts of questions about why God doesn't heal more often. We will get to those questions a bit later in this chapter, but I don't want us to miss this crucial point: *God's compassion moves Him to heal.* When that truth begins to sink in, we realize the importance of this continuing today. Healing prayer enables us to demonstrate the compassion of Jesus toward those who are suffering.

Jesus Multiplied His Healing Ministry

I realize I just made a huge leap with that last sentence. It's one thing to assert that healing was an important aspect of *Jesus'* ministry. Most every Christian wholeheartedly agrees with that. The controversy arises when we talk about healing happening today. Should the ministry of the Spirit in our lives involve healing, or was that primarily reserved for Jesus and the apostles?

What makes this question particularly difficult is our tendency to base our theology on our experience. We look around us and do not see the level of miracles that occurred in Jesus' ministry or through the apostles, so we conclude that God doesn't regularly do this anymore. He might occasionally perform a miraculous healing, but we shouldn't expect this to happen very often.

Some argue that Jesus' healing ministry (and later the apostles) was reserved for that particular season of time, as a way of authenticating the Messiah and the establishment of the church. Since we now have the Bible in our possession, frequent, miraculous healings are not needed today. While I understand how someone might reach that conclusion, the New Testament describes a very different perspective on healing, revealing that this work of the Spirit is intended to be a very natural and normal part of the Christian experience.

We have seen how healing played a significant role in the life of Jesus. What's fascinating is that Jesus was not content to keep this ministry to Himself. In Luke 9:1, 6 we read, "When Jesus had called the Twelve together, he gave them power and authority to drive out all demons and cure diseases .... so they set out and went from village to village, proclaiming the good news and healing people everywhere."

So now thirteen people were involved in healing — Jesus and his twelve disciples. But He didn't stop there:

> After this the Lord appointed seventy-two others and sent them two by two ahead of him to every town and place where he was about to go. He

told them ... "Heal the sick who are there and tell them, 'The kingdom of God has come near to you.'"   Luke 10:1-2, 9

Notice, we've gone from one to twelve to seventy-two. We don't even know the names of these seventy-two. Not apostles, they were ordinary folks like you and me who wanted to follow Jesus. So Jesus sent them out to pray for the sick in the power of the Spirit, declaring in word and deed that the kingdom of God had come near. Jesus had no desire to keep this ministry of healing to Himself. The circle of the Spirit's activity was ever-widening ... and He wasn't finished.

In Acts 6:8 we learn that Stephen, who was not an apostle, "performed great wonders and signs among the people." That phrase "wonders and signs" refers to miracles like healing and deliverance. A few chapters later we read about Philip — another ordinary guy — who traveled to Samaria, and

Evidence in the New Testament as well as history reveals God's desire for the ministry of healing to be a normal part of our experience as Christians.

guess what happened? "With shrieks, impure spirits came out of many, and many who were paralyzed or lame were healed" (Acts 8:7). Later in his letter to the Galatians, Paul acknowledged that miracles were regularly occurring among them (see Galatians 3:5).

Clearly the ministry of healing was not reserved for the apostles alone but became a normal part of church life in the New Testament, continuing for several hundred years. Dr. Ramsay MacMullan, a professor of history and classics at Yale University, explains that early Christians "took miracles quite for granted. That was the general starting point. Not to believe them would have made you seem more than odd."[1]

He also declared that the primary reason Rome converted to Christianity was because of the church's involvement in healing and exorcism.[2] Evidence in the New Testament as well as history reveals God's desire for the ministry of healing to be a normal part of our experience as Christians.

The Ministry of Healing Can Be an Everyday Part of Your Life

So what would it look like to make the ministry of healing a normal part of our experience as Christians? It's nothing complicated. *Pray regularly for those around you who are sick.* That's it. Make healing prayer an ordinary response to sickness. This morning my wife had a migraine. She texted me asking me to pray for healing, which I did.

For years, Raylene and I have modeled this with our children, praying for each other when family members are sick. One evening when Raylene was pregnant with our second son, she experienced some intense back pain. As she rested on the recliner, our two-year-old daughter Erin asked if she could pray for Mommy. "Of course," Raylene replied.

Erin immediately placed her hand on Raylene's back, *Thank you, Jesus, for the food.* That was the only prayer she knew at the time ... but at least she was learning how praying for the hurting is a normal part of walking with Jesus.

Often in Christian circles when we hear someone share about a physical or emotional issue, we tell them we will pray for them (which may or may not happen). Why don't we just stop right then and pray for the person, asking God to heal?

A few weeks ago, I flew home from a conference with a pastor friend. On the plane, I noticed he was wiggling and moving the fingers on his right hand. When I asked him what was going on, he explained that he had injured his hand a few weeks before and had since been unable to tie his shoes or do other hands-on tasks. I could tell he felt discouraged.

In the past, I probably would have responded by expressing sympathy and promising to pray for him. This time I actually prayed. After we arrived at the airport, we walked together toward the baggage claim area. But first, I asked if I could pray for him right then. He readily agreed, so we stopped in the middle of the airport.

As I gently placed my hand on his injured hand, I prayed, *Father, thank you for Your love for Kevin. I ask You to heal his hand. I pray that You fill this area of his body with Your Spirit and remove the pain. Restore his hand to function the way You created it to function. Freedom of movement without pain, we ask in Jesus' name.*

We then said our goodbyes and went our separate ways. A few days later, he emailed me and said that his hand no longer hurt. The pain had left soon after our prayer, and he was once again able to type on the computer and tie his shoes. How cool is that?

A few months ago after one of our worship services, a woman in our congregation mentioned to me that she had recently injured her knee. The pain was excruciating, making it difficult to climb the stairs or get in and out of bed. She expressed her anxiety about her MRI that was scheduled later that week.

I offered to pray for her right then and decided to pray not only for her anxiety but also for her physical healing. After the prayer, she thanked me and went home.

When I saw her the next week, she smiled and said, "Remember praying for me last week?"

"Of course I do. How are you feeling?"

"As you prayed, I began to feel tingly and warm. I felt my muscles relax. When I got ready for bed that night, I could actually get changed. I called out to my husband and told him to watch me as I picked up my leg and flexed it. No pain. I got into bed. No pain. I woke up with no pain."

Can you imagine what might happen in our lives and in our churches if our instinctive response to someone in physical pain was to pray for healing for them at that moment?

What an amazing God we serve! All of that resulted from a five-minute prayer after a worship service. Can you imagine what might happen in our lives and in our churches if our instinctive response to someone in physical pain was to pray for healing for them at that moment? We can *say* we believe that God heals, but why not actually pray for it? I have noticed an interesting correlation: the more often I pray for healing for people, the more frequently healings happen. Why wouldn't we want that?

But Why Doesn't God Heal More Often?

How wonderful to hear examples like that. But honestly, for every story of healing, I can probably name ten people who received healing prayer and didn't see any noticeable improvement. What do we do with that? I think this question, more than any other, causes us to hesitate when praying for others or even asking for prayer for ourselves. What if God doesn't heal? If we believe He desires to heal and has the power to do so, how do we process this when our prayers don't result in healing?

For our family, this is not just a theoretical or theological question. It is a very personal one. As mentioned in an earlier chapter, our youngest son was born with significant cognitive and verbal problems. At thirteen years old, he still can't put a complete sentence together, bathe himself, tie his shoes or consistently write his full name. For thirteen years, we and numerous others have earnestly asked God to heal our son ... and have seen little improvement. So what do we do with that?

Many times we have felt like throwing our hands in the air and concluding, *What's the use? Why even pray? Why continue to pray for healing?* In our darker moments, we have wondered if God even cares. Maybe you have felt the same thing after praying for a loved one to be healed of a terminal illness and then watching them die.

This deeply felt question significantly shapes our attitude toward healing, making us hesitant, even skeptical, about God's love and His power — which certainly isn't God's desire. As we have seen, Scripture encourages the ministry of healing to be a normal part of our Christian experience. So what are we to do?

We desperately need a theology big enough to simultaneously embrace two biblical realities:

Because God desires to heal, we can boldly pray for healing.

And

Sometimes, for reasons beyond our understanding, God chooses not to heal, and we can trust Him anyway.

Both of these are essential and biblical truths to embrace at the same time. Theologians refer to this tension as the "now and the not yet" of the kingdom. In one sense, the kingdom of God is here. When Jesus began His ministry, He declared that "the kingdom of God has come near" (Mark 1:15) and then demonstrated the presence of the kingdom by healing people and delivering them. Today, when we pray for the sick and see them healed, the now of the kingdom is on display.

However, this kingdom is not fully here. We live in a fallen world where sin and evil are still active. This curse won't be fully reversed until we get to heaven—when God's kingdom will be fully present. On that day, there will be no more pain or death (Revelation 21:4). Sounds awesome … but we're not yet there. So we live in the tension between the now and the not yet of the kingdom.

If we want to grow in our experience of healing, we must simultaneously embrace both of these kingdom realities—that God desires to heal AND that sometimes He chooses not to.

If we want to grow in our experience of healing, we must simultaneously embrace both of these kingdom realities—that God desires to heal AND that sometimes He chooses not to. Paul certainly embraced both at the same time. In Galatians 3:5, Paul acknowledged that miracles happened in the churches in that region (the now of the kingdom). However, later in this same book, Paul wrote,

> As you know, it was because of an illness that I first preached the gospel to you, and even though my illness was a trial to you, you did not treat me with contempt or scorn. Instead, you

welcomed me as if I were an angel of God, as if I were Christ Jesus himself.   Galatians 4:13-14

Paul acknowledged that "because of an illness" God opened a door for him to preach the gospel there. Evidently God didn't immediately heal him, for Paul described how his illness was a trial to them (the not yet of the kingdom). Does this illness minimize the reality of God's power and desire to heal? Absolutely not. It does, however, require a big enough theological framework to include not only God's desire to heal but also His ability to use suffering for His sovereign, loving purposes.

In order to grow in the ministry of healing, we must simultaneously embrace both of these truths ... which isn't easy to do. We as Christians tend to embrace one of these and not the other, and the impact can be quite significant.

Some of Us Insist on Healing Now

Some of us focus only on the now of the kingdom — that healing is ours to claim today, *if* we pray with enough faith. While I admire this perspective's bold faith and expectancy, it unwittingly places the burden for healing on *our* shoulders. If healing doesn't happen, we must have sin in our life or perhaps we didn't pray with enough faith.

Do you see the potential dangers here? If we're not careful, our prayers will become attempts to coerce God to do what we want (sort of like the prophets of Baal in 1 Kings 18). What if God has a larger purpose we don't understand (like Paul's illness in Galatians 4)?

In addition, focusing only on the now of the kingdom can cause significant emotional and spiritual turmoil for those who aren't healed. If it is *always*

God's will to heal and I'm not healed, there must be something wrong with me.

A few years ago, a door-to-door salesperson stopped by our house to sell us a vacuum cleaner. In the course of the conversation, she observed our son Josh's disability and began lecturing my wife on how God would heal our son if we just had enough faith. This woman had no idea the years of earnest praying we had done. All she had was her formula for healing that she wielded without any compassion or willingness to enter into our pain. Ironically, I'm sure she felt that her faith was quite large, when in reality her faith was too small, unable to include a God who, for some loving purpose, might choose not to heal.

Some of Us Are Stuck in the Not Yet

On the other end of the spectrum, focusing only on the not yet of the kingdom also results in spiritual danger. Many Christians settle into this perspective without even realizing it. We say that God has the power to heal, but rarely if ever *pray* for Him to do so. And when we do pray for healing, we pray without any sense of boldness or expectancy, thus betraying our true belief.

I recently heard someone pray for a person who was sick. They prayed for the doctors. They prayed for comfort and strength for the person who was ill, but they seemed unable to bring themselves to actually pray for God to heal this person. If we're not careful, we can settle into a functional deism, where we say we believe in God's power to heal, but we rarely if ever pray boldly and expectantly for healing to happen.

In his excellent book, *Authority to Heal*, Ken Blue tells of meeting a seminary student who had suffered a stroke and was paralyzed on the left side of his body. When Blue offered to pray for him, this young man named Richard thanked him but politely declined, explaining how he had grown closer to God in the paralysis. Ken agreed that God had used this but suggested that God might want to also bring value out of healing him. Richard continued to decline any prayer, saying, "I don't want to miss out on anything God wants to teach me through this."

Then Ken asked a very interesting question: "Do you go to physical therapy to improve your condition?" The young man said, "Of course." To which Ken responded, "Why would you accept improvement for your condition through therapy but not through prayer?" After a long pause, he shrugged his one good shoulder and said, "I don't know."[3]

What an interesting response. This young man obviously thought it was God's will for him to go to therapy to improve his condition. Why not also receive healing prayer to improve his condition?

I'm guessing that a number of you reading this page have fallen into a similar belief system. You regularly see doctors or take medicine to alleviate some physical ailment, but you have never asked anyone to pray specifically and earnestly for healing for your condition. If this is the case, your theology of healing isn't big enough. You readily embrace the second truth mentioned earlier regarding God's sovereign purposes, but you do not really believe the first truth—that God desires to heal.

Why Not Both?

Why can't we embrace both of these truths? Why can't we pray with boldness and expectancy for the sick, earnestly asking God to heal AND also leave the results in His hands, trusting His purposes either way? To do so leaves plenty of room for mystery in this whole area of healing prayer. We don't understand God's ways but we can trust Him. We don't understand God's power but we can ask Him to heal.

We don't understand God's ways but we can trust Him. We don't understand God's power but we can ask Him to heal.

One thing I do know: If we don't ask for healing, it won't happen. "You do not have because you do not ask God" (James 4:2).

My wife and I will continue to ask boldly for Joshua's healing, and yet at the same time we are continually amazed at how God uses our son to bless others. Someday, Joshua will be healed — either in this life or the next. Until then, we will continually and boldly ask for healing *and* we will continue to trust God's heart and His loving purposes.

To some, this may feel like an unnecessary tension. To others it may seem like a lack of faith. But to us, it has been a critical foundation for growing in the Spirit's ministry of healing. It really is God's desire to heal ... and we get to be a part of sharing His heart and compassion with a hurting world.

Want to learn more about how you can grow in this wonderful and normal part of the Christian life? Then keep reading...

HOLY SPIRIT LABORATORY

Think of the physical ailments you have recently or currently struggle with—like headaches, acid reflux, a cold, allergies, ringing in your ears, back pain, high blood pressure, etc. For how many of these have you asked someone to offer a bold prayer for healing on your behalf? Ask someone to pray for healing for whatever physical ailments you are experiencing.

If you are hesitant to do this, ask yourself why that is. Do you not believe God wants your condition to improve? I'm guessing that for most of us, we have seen a doctor or taken medicine to alleviate our ailment, which is fine. Medicine is a God-given vehicle through which healing can happen. However, why would we also not pray for healing as well?

Chapter Nine

How to Pray for the Sick

—ᨓ—

Recently the Vatican officially recognized a miracle of healing that occurred in Colorado to a 4-year-old boy with a very serious intestinal condition. While doctors couldn't figure out why this little boy was getting sick 10 to 12 times a day, two nuns prayed for him and his condition improved dramatically. When I read about this in the newspaper, I rejoiced in God's power. And yet, one aspect of this story did trouble me. This miracle happened 15 years ago! Is that how we should view healing—as a once every decade occurrence, or might the Spirit of God want to do this more frequently?

As we saw in the last chapter, the Bible clearly shows that God continues to heal and has delegated this ministry to the church. Healing should be a normal part of our Christian experience. So how can we more effectively pray for the sick? That's what we are going to talk about in this chapter, offering a practical guide to the ministry of healing prayer.

God Likes to Multitask

In order to effectively pray for the sick, we must first recognize the complexity of human beings. God created us not only with a physical dimension but also a spiritual and emotional dimension as well. These facets do not exist as independent silos, but are interconnected realities. So as we pray for people's physical healing, we must be attentive to their emotional and spiritual lives as well.

In Luke 5:20, Jesus said to a paralytic, "Friend, your sins are forgiven," and then healed him (see also John 5:13–15). God's spiritual forgiveness helped pave the way for physical healing. Sometimes physical symptoms (such as insomnia, digestive pain, headaches, etc.) are rooted in an emotional issue (such as forgiveness or shame.) To only pray for physical healing without an awareness of these other factors may cause us to miss the core issue.

As we pray for people's physical healing, we must be attentive to their emotional and spiritual lives as well.

At times, a sickness may be the result of an open door given to the enemy's work in a person's life. In Luke 13:11, Luke described a woman who had "been crippled by a spirit for eighteen years. She was bent over and could not straighten up at all." Her physical condition was directly connected to a deeper issue. As Jesus delivered her from the evil spirit, she experienced physical healing as well.

As we pray for someone, we may discern that some activity in their past opened a door for the enemy's influence (for example, involvement in the occult, séances, sexual immorality, etc. See Neil Anderson's *The Bondage Breaker* for a more complete list and strategy)[1].

By specifically confessing and renouncing these activities, the person can be freed from the enemy's foothold.

We desperately need the Spirit of God to guide us as we pray for people, so that we can discern the root issues and pray more effectively. Listening to the Spirit is essential in any healing prayer opportunity.

We Need to Pray with Faith

Another essential factor in effectively praying for the sick is faith. Even a cursory glance at Jesus' healing ministry displays the critical importance of faith (see Matthew 9:20–22, Mark 5:36 for a few examples). In Mark 6:5–6 we read that Jesus "could not do any miracles there, except lay his hands on a few sick people *Faith is essential as we pray for the sick.* and heal them. He was amazed at their lack of faith." You may want to read that verse one more time. Even Jesus could not do any miracles because of their lack of faith. No question, faith is essential as we pray for the sick.

But what does that kind of faith specifically look like? Our answer to that question will significantly impact how we pray for people. Before we talk about genuine faith, let's look at some *unhealthy* ways faith is expressed.

Forceful faith

In this approach, we measure the effectiveness of our faith by how forcefully we pray. The more decibels used, the more powerful our prayer. We beg and plead, believing that God's responsiveness depends on our passion and intensity. While I'm certainly not opposed to earnest intercession (as we will see in a moment), the danger relates to our perception of God. We lose sight of God's heart to heal and instead feel that we must coerce and convince Him to act. Is that really the God we serve?

Formulaic faith

A second unhealthy approach turns faith into a formula. *If you just do this, this, and this, God will heal you.* The specifics vary—claim this verse, give this amount of money, or fast for a certain length of time. In this approach, we reduce God to a cosmic vending machine. We just need to figure out what to put in the machine so that we receive the product we want. Notice the responsibility for healing ultimately rests upon us, rather than God. If healing doesn't happen, a person is left wondering what they did wrong. They blame themselves.

Faking-It faith

A friend of mine once attended a motivational, self-help seminar focused on achieving success. He later summarized the basic teaching: "Fake it 'til you make it." In other words, stay positive and upbeat, no matter what. That accurately describes how we sometimes approach healing and faith: *Once you receive healing prayer, thank God for healing you, even if you don't feel any better. Don't let doubt creep in. Just keep believing.*

This can create a fake-it atmosphere in the church where, after receiving healing prayer, a person doesn't want to admit they still don't feel well. To do so, they are told, is to be speaking forth negativity and unbelief. While I understand the power of the spoken word and the importance of expectancy, this approach can foster an unhealthy, inauthentic church culture where people feel uncomfortable acknowledging the truth about their physical condition.

Faith is Childlike Trust in Our Heavenly Father

So what does genuine faith look like? If it's not a means of coercing God, nor a formula for getting God to act, what is it? Look at how Ken Blue answers this question:

The faith to be healed and to pray for the sick is nothing other than childlike trust in the loving character and purpose of our Heavenly Father. … True Christian faith in all its expressions looks away from self to God and what he has done for us in Jesus Christ. The real question is not: "Do I believe strongly enough to be healed or to pray for the sick?" but, "Is God the sort of person I can trust, and am I willing to be open to his love?"[2]

I love that! This definition removes faith from any formulaic or coercive context and places it where it needs to be — firmly rooted in our love relationship with our heavenly Father. He delights when we come to Him and ask. He wants us to trust His heart and His love as we make our requests before Him. Our God is not a distant, uncaring ogre in the sky whom we must convince to act in this situation. Rather,

Our God is not a distant, uncaring ogre in the sky whom we must convince to act in [our] situation.

He is our loving Father who urges us to ask boldly for healing and trust His love for us and for the person for whom we are praying.

Faith defined this way frees us from worrying about whether or not we're doing it right. The key question is: Are we approaching our Father in childlike faith, trusting His character and His loving purposes? If so, we're praying in faith.

So how much faith is enough? Remember Jesus' incredible statement in Matthew 17:20 — that if we have faith the size of a mustard seed, we can move mountains. A mustard seed is one of the smallest of all seeds. Jesus wants us to understand that faith is more about quality than quantity. Do you truly believe that God really can heal? Can you pray with expectancy, knowing the heart of our heavenly Father and then leaving the results to Him? If so, you have the faith to pray for healing.

This discussion raises a very important question: Exactly *whose* faith is important—the person praying OR the person receiving prayer? Yes! Sometimes Jesus healed in response to the faith of the sick person. But other times, the Bible emphasizes the faith of those praying for healing (see James 5:16). In Luke 5, Jesus healed a paralytic in response to the faith of those who brought the sick man to Him. "When Jesus saw *their* faith" … He healed the man (Luke 5:20, my emphasis). No doubt, faith is essential, but the location of that faith doesn't seem to be the emphasis.

Not long ago a woman in our church approached a prayer team, asking for prayer regarding an upcoming surgery. Nervous about the anesthesia, she requested their prayers. As the team *Healing happens* prayed for her, they felt led to *most often in* pray not only for the anesthesia *community.* but also for healing so that surgery wouldn't be necessary. Days later, as she was being wheeled down to the surgery, the doctor asked her how her leg felt. When she told him that she had no pain, he asked, "Why then are we doing surgery?" and he sent her home. This woman didn't even have the faith to ask for healing prayer, but those praying for her did. God responded to *their* faith.

All these examples reveal an important truth: *Healing happens most often in community.* When I pray for my own healing, I rarely see results. Faith flourishes best in community—when we acknowledge our need and ask others to pray for us. That requires a healthy dose of humility, and let's be honest. Sometimes we are too proud and self-sufficient to ask others to pray for us. Could that be one reason we don't experience more healing? God wants our faith to be expressed in the context of community, where we can acknowledge our need to other people. That humble act of asking for prayer becomes a significant demonstration of faith.

Jesus Has Given You Authority to Heal

In addition to understanding the nature and importance of faith, we must also understand the nature and importance of *authority* as it relates to healing prayer. When Jesus sent out His followers in Luke 9, we are told that "He gave them power and authority to drive out all demons and to cure diseases" (Luke 9:1). Power AND authority. What's the difference?

Let's say you're in a park and a stranger tells you to leave. You realize this person is physically larger and stronger than you, so you leave. That's power. Now let's change the scenario a bit. What if this stranger is shorter and skinnier than you, but happens to be wearing a police uniform. When he tells you to leave, you leave. That's authority.

When Jesus encountered people suffering from sickness, He often responded with authority. For instance, in Luke 4, Jesus is asked to pray for Peter's mother-in-law, who suffered from a high fever. "So he bent over her and rebuked the fever, and it left her" (Luke 4:39). Notice, He didn't *pray* for her healing. He spoke directly to the fever, and it left her. In Luke 5, Jesus says, "Be clean," to a leper (Luke 5:13) and "take your mat" to a paralytic (Luke 5:24), both of whom were immediately healed.

One of the most eye-opening discoveries for me when studying Jesus' ministry of healing prayer was how rarely Jesus actually *prayed* for healing. Most often,

He spoke a command and the illness left. Jesus wielded tremendous authority when ministering to the sick. Even more amazing is the fact that He then delegated this authority to His followers. As we saw a moment ago in Luke 9:1, Jesus gave His twelve disciples "power and authority" to heal. Later, He gave this same authority to 72 other followers (see Luke 10:17, 19). How amazing to realize that Jesus delegated His authority to us to use when praying for others.

How amazing to realize that Jesus delegated His authority to us to use when praying for others.

So what does this look like practically speaking? I'm certainly not encouraging us to walk around telling everyone in a wheelchair to get up and walk. Enough damage has been done by so-called faith healers who practice healing in this way. But I do believe we *can* more intentionally utilize our God-given authority when praying for the sick … without being forceful or weird.

For example, sometimes when I pray for someone for healing, I ask God to heal them. *"Lord pour out Your Spirit and heal Steve of his back pain. We ask You to fill his body with Your power and heal him completely."* But other times in a similar situation, I pray with more authority. *"In the name of Jesus, I speak to this back pain and command you to stop. Muscles, relax in Jesus' name. Spine, come into alignment in the name of Jesus."*

I know this probably makes some of you feel uncomfortable. I get that. I felt a bit uncomfortable the first few times I prayed this way. But I have seen God do amazing work in response to this more authoritative approach. I'm not saying this is the *only* way to pray for healing, but it can be a legitimate option when ministering to the sick.

So how do we know whether we should pray for God to heal, or pray with Jesus' authority by commanding the sickness to leave? The Holy Spirit. As we are attentive to His presence and His leading, He will show us how to pray, giving us the insight we need.

Here's an Easy Model for Healing Prayer

One of the best ways to learn to do something is by watching someone model it for us. I recently took my son to a tennis lesson and videotaped the session so we could later see how the tennis pro struck the ball with his forehand and backhand. Without a helpful pattern or example, we are left trying to figure it out on our own.

The same is true in healing prayer. In this section, I will present a basic model that has been used by a number of people who minister effectively in healing prayer.[1] Do not view this model as a legalistic formula. Rather, feel free to adapt it to fit each situation.

Step One: Interview

Whenever you pray for someone's healing, initially take a brief amount of time to find out more about their condition. Begin by asking questions like, *"What would you like us to pray for? Where do you feel pain? Is there a specific diagnosis? When did the pain start? What other treatments have you received for this?"* By gathering this information, you can pray more accurately. However, try not to let this turn into a full-blown medical evaluation. Keep it simple.

In this process, always communicate love and warmth to the person. If they seem anxious about receiving prayer, try to alleviate their anxiety. Often I will say something like, *"Don't feel any need to do anything as we pray. Just receive. If you do sense anything happening, please let us know. Otherwise, just relax and receive all the Lord has for you."*

I also typically ask the person if it's okay that we lay our hands on them at times during the prayer session. The laying on of hands is a biblical practice (see Luke 4:40, Acts 8:18, Hebrews 6:1-3), providing a tangible, compassionate connection with the person as well as sometimes serving as a conduit for the Spirit's power. For these reasons, I encourage those praying to lay hands on the person receiving prayer.

Step Two: Invite the Holy Spirit's Presence

The Spirit's presence is critical in our ability to pray effectively. We need Him to lead us and reveal to us how we should pray. Because of this, I like to begin with a prayer of blessing. *"Father, thank You for Maria. I pray that she will receive all that You have for her today. Fill her with Your peace."* I then welcome the Spirit's presence. *"Holy Spirit, we welcome You to come and fill us with Your presence. We pray that You would show us how to pray in this situation. Reveal to us anything that would be helpful in our praying."*

After that simple prayer, take some time to wait on the Lord. Quiet your heart and see if He guides you in any way.

Step Three: Pray as the Spirit Leads

As you begin sensing the Spirit's leading, pray according to the direction He gives you. You may feel rising up within you a bold, faith-filled prayer for healing. Pray that. You may sense a need to speak directly to the condition in the authority of Jesus and command it to leave. If so, go for it. Let the Spirit lead you as you pray and then do what He asks.

He may lead you to anoint this person with oil, as James 5:14-16 encourages. The Spirit may prompt you to lay hands on a particular part of the person's body (ask permission of course), or may bring to mind a word, a Scripture or a picture to share with the person. Perhaps issues of unforgiveness or spiritual warfare surface. The key is to rely on the Spirit's leading as you pray.

At times, it may be helpful to stop and ask the person how they are doing or if they feel anything happening. When we ask this question, we want to make sure people don't feel any pressure to answer a particular way—i.e. to say they are feeling better, when in reality they are not. Assure them that it's okay if they are not feeling anything specific. You want them to be honest and open so you can pray accordingly. If they feel the pain lessening, continue the prayer approach you have been utilizing. If they don't sense anything, that's okay. You may want to once again quiet your heart, asking for the Spirit to lead you as you pray.

We must remember that healing is God's responsibility. Our job is to pray in faith and to trust Him.

The other day, a few of our prayer team members prayed for a woman who had injured her ankle at work a few months earlier and was experiencing a great deal of pain. After a few minutes of praying with authority for healing, we stopped and asked her, "How is your ankle? Are you feeling anything?" She responded by saying, "The pain is significantly less." That encouraged us, so we continued to pray. Soon, she began moving her foot around and was able to walk without her crutches.

I readily admit that stopping to ask this question is extremely difficult for me. I'm afraid the person will say that nothing is happening, which will then make me feel like a failure. However, in those moments of fear, we must remember that healing is God's responsibility. Our job is to pray in faith and to trust Him. We then leave the results in His hands. The pressure's off.

Not long ago we prayed for a dear woman in our congregation who for years has suffered from a debilitating neurological condition brought on by an unexpected reaction to over–the-counter medication. We earnestly prayed for several minutes, often stopping to ask if she felt any improvement. She didn't. To this day, her condition has not improved, but we continue to take every opportunity to pray for her healing.

Step Four: Bring Closure

When you sense the prayer time is finished, take a moment to thank God for what He has done. Pray a blessing on the person and ask the Spirit to continue His work in their life.

After this prayer of blessing, dialogue with the person about what happened and offer any counsel for next steps. If they experienced some healing, rejoice with them in God's provision. If they did not perceive that God was healing them, encourage them to continue praying and asking for people to pray for them. Remind them that sometimes healing happens over time. And of course, affirm to them the reality of God's loving purposes for their lives.

Let me reiterate: this model is not intended to be a legalistic formula but can be a helpful guide as we practice healing prayer. The model is simple enough to be done in a few minutes, but significant enough to guide you in a much longer, more intense prayer session if needed.

In our church, we have healing prayer teams available during and after worship services. We also offer a ministry called "soaking prayer." People can sign up for an hour-long time slot on a Sunday afternoon to receive listening prayer and/or healing prayer from a prayer team.

What I love about healing prayer is that it can be a normal part of our everyday lives. Whenever we encounter someone who is not feeling well, we can offer to pray for them. I recently heard author and speaker Michael Evans describe a prayer opportunity that occurred while traveling on an airplane. During the flight, one of the flight attendants apologized over the intercom for the delay in bringing out the drinks and snacks.

She explained that she was in a great deal of pain due to an abscessed tooth. A few minutes later when she stopped at Michael's row to take drink orders, he quietly asked her if she would mind if he prayed for her tooth. She welcomed the idea, so he gently placed his hand on her cheek and offered up a prayer for her healing. She thanked him, and then said, "I think it's feeling better." Within minutes, she was back to her normal self. Every time she walked by his seat, she told him that her pain was gone. Soon others sitting around Michael wanted him to pray for them as well!

What might happen if you and I lived our lives freely offering Jesus' healing power to others—even being willing to stop and pray for anyone in need of healing? I realize this initially may feel awkward, but most of time, people in pain are very willing to receive prayer. Why not ask them if you can pray for them?

You may be wondering, *What if nothing happens when I pray?* Here's what I've found: no matter what, this person will feel loved and cared for by you. Even if there is no immediate healing, they have experienced the touch of Jesus in your willingness to care for them. Either way, Jesus wins.

HOLY SPIRIT LABORATORY

Situation one: The next time someone in your life is experiencing a minor physical discomfort (cold, flu, headache, stomach pain, etc.), offer to pray for them right there. Let the Spirit lead you as you pray for healing.

Situation two: Think of someone in your life who experiences a chronic physical condition (asthma, back pain, migraines, insomnia, etc.). Offer to pray for them about their condition.

Chapter Ten

How the Spirit Can Energize
Your Prayer Life

—ɱ—

M y teenage son and I recently traveled to Europe
to serve at a Christian leadership conference. In
planning the trip, we decided to leave a day early and
spend time in Venice, Italy. Initially this sounded like
a great idea, hanging out with my son in an incredibly
beautiful location.

But the closer the trip got, the more anxious I felt.
In all of my previous overseas trips, someone else orga-
nized the details about transportation from the airport,
sites to visit, how to get there, etc. But this time, I was in
charge. There was no one to greet us at the airport. No
one to explain how and where we could find a shuttle to
our hotel. No one to help us figure out how to exchange
money and not get ripped off. Different country.
Different language. No one familiar. Thus my stress.

When we arrived at the airport, we found an ATM
and exchanged some money so we could call the hotel.
I found a pay phone (to avoid exorbitant cell phone
charges) but couldn't figure out how it worked since

everything was in Italian. Finally we got through to the hotel, where an irritated front desk person directed me — in broken English — to go outside the airport and look for a gray van. Sounded simple. We quickly walked outside, only to realize we didn't know where we were supposed to wait for this gray van or when it would arrive.

After standing for several minutes and seeing nothing even remotely gray, I was at a loss for what to do. In desperation, I found a young man nearby and explained our situation, asking if he could help us. Immediately, he took out his cell phone and called our hotel. After rattling off some very rapid Italian, he put away his phone and explained that we were supposed to wait on the upstairs level rather than at arrivals. We headed upstairs and within minutes were on our way. Frustration, stress, panic — all completely removed the moment we found someone willing and able to help us. Help is an amazing thing especially when we find ourselves at the end of our resources in the midst of a strange place.

Help, I'm Praying!

I'm guessing most of us would readily admit that sometimes prayer feels a bit like traveling to a foreign country. We make time to pray, arriving in a quiet place to spend time with God, expectantly hoping for a meaningful encounter with Him. We have resources in hand but soon realize we're not exactly sure how this "pay phone" works. Even when we get through, the conversation feels a bit awkward and distant. We long to experience the depths of prayer that other people talk about, but feel uncertain as to what we are doing. Sometimes we give up in frustration. Other times, we continue to "stand there", but secretly wonder if we're even "standing" in the right place. What we need is help—a person who can assist us in this strange and wonderful experience of prayer.

In light of that, look carefully at the apostle Paul's incredible words to us:

> In the same way, the Spirit helps us in our weakness. We do not know what we ought to pray for, but the Spirit himself intercedes for us through wordless groans. And he who searches our hearts knows the mind of the Spirit, because the Spirit intercedes for God's people in accordance with the will of God.   Romans 8:26–27

The apostle Paul describes an amazing reality. When we are in the midst of suffering and difficulty, not knowing even how to put into words what is on our hearts, the Spirit of God eagerly steps in and helps. He does so by praying for us, interceding before the Father on our behalf. This is no casual, indifferent intercession—"God, please help them." Rather, the Spirit prays for us with "wordless groans." The Spirit feels our pain, our groans (see verse 23), our longings—all of which move Him to pray earnestly and passionately on our behalf.

When we are in the midst of suffering and difficulty, not knowing even how to put into words what is on our hearts, the Spirit of God eagerly steps in and helps.

Have you ever felt so overwhelmed by circumstances and difficulties that you knew you wanted and needed to pray, but once alone with the Father, all you could express were groans of pain? Perhaps the anguish of an adult son or daughter making decisions that break your heart, or the sting of rejection, or the pang of loneliness. God wants you to know, not only that He is with you, but also that His Spirit feels your pain and earnestly groans in prayer to the Father on your behalf. In those moments, you don't have to try and come up with the right words. You can offer the Lord your groans, and know that the Spirit groans with you. The Spirit helps in your weakness.

The Spirit Can Infuse Your Entire Prayer Life

The Spirit assists us in prayer, not only in times of weakness. In Ephesians 6:18, Paul urges us to "Pray in the Spirit on all occasions with all kinds of prayers and requests." God intends the Spirit to play an integral part of our *entire* prayer life. So what does praying in the Spirit look like?

To pray in the Spirit means to pray with an intentional attentiveness to the Spirit.

To pray in the Spirit means to pray with an intentional attentiveness to the Spirit. He longs to play a vital part in our prayers, leading us in how we should pray. That little two letter word "in" (as in "pray in the Spirit") reminds us that prayer is ultimately about *relationship* with God. Communion with Him. Without this dynamic, our prayer lives become little more than a one-way conversation where we're doing all the talking.

A friend of mine described a recent experience in what he thought was a budding romantic relationship. After spending many conversations listening to this woman talk, my friend tried to share a bit about himself. Immediately her eyes glazed over and she seemed bored. The moment he finished sharing, she jumped in to a topic on her mind. He now wonders how far this friendship can ever really develop.

Deep relationships involve two-way communication. Prayer functions the same way. As we explored in previous chapters, the Spirit desires to speak to us and lead us as we pray. His promptings, His voice, His presence bring a relational reality to our praying. When our prayer lives consist of doing all the talking without ever stopping to listen or be attentive to the Spirit, we're probably not praying in the Spirit.

In Revelation 1:10 John writes, "On the Lord's Day I was in the Spirit and I heard behind me a loud voice." As John worshipped the Lord that day, God gave him this incredible vision. But notice his heart posture when it occurred—"I was in the Spirit." In other words, he was attentive to and aware of the Spirit's presence. In that place, God spoke and directed John's prayer time.

When I teach people about prayer, I like to use the Lord's Prayer as a model. The prayer Jesus gave us has been a wonderful help for me—not to recite word for word, but rather as a pattern for my prayer experience. Here's the diagram I often use when teaching this[1]:

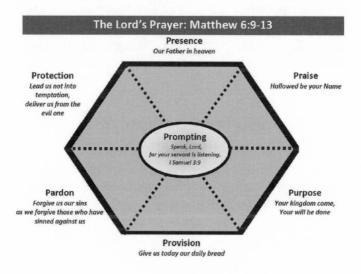

The Lord's Prayer: Matthew 6:9-13

Presence
Our Father in heaven

Protection
Lead us not into temptation, deliver us from the evil one

Praise
Hallowed be your Name

Prompting
Speak, Lord, for your servant is listening.
I Samuel 3:9

Pardon
Forgive us our sins as we forgive those who have sinned against us

Purpose
Your kingdom come, Your will be done

Provision
Give us today our daily bread

I encourage people to start at the top and begin praying each section. For instance, at Presence ("Our Father in heaven") people can take a few minutes to enjoy their relationship with God as Father. In Purpose ("Your kingdom come"), people can spend a few minutes praying for any area in which they long to see God's kingdom (His power, His reign) released. Using this model helps us experience the "all kinds of prayer" that Paul refers to in Ephesians 6:18, including praise, confession, intercession, spiritual warfare, etc.

We want our entire prayer life to be in the Spirit, attentive to and aware of the Spirit as we pray.

But notice the center of the diagram — Prompting. As I pray through these sections, I want to be attentive to the Spirit, prompted by Him in that particular area. For instance when praying the Pardon section, I often ask the Holy Spirit to bring to mind any sin I need to confess or any person I need to forgive. I then wait and listen.

We want our entire prayer life to be in the Spirit, attentive to and aware of the Spirit as we pray. The result will be a deepening experiencing of friendship with Jesus.

HOLY SPIRIT LABORATORY

Pray through the Lord's Prayer as just described. Start at the top with Presence and then pray each section. In each, be attentive to how the Spirit may lead you in that area.

Tongues: Another Kind of Praying in the Spirit

All of this discussion about experiencing the Spirit in our prayers raises an issue worth exploring: speaking in tongues (or spiritual language). This topic has been quite controversial and stirred much conflict in the body of Christ. Some make it a requirement for Spirit fullness, a mark of maturity. Others, out of fear or frustration, choose to ignore the topic all together. Either way, speaking in tongues has been a source of significant tension over the centuries. Is there a way to approach this subject without drawing lines in the sand? Thankfully, yes.

In 1 Corinthians 14, Paul talks about this subject in a thorough and balanced way. When we truly understand what he is saying, we immediately realize this topic need not cause conflict or tension; we can actually relax about it! So let's look at Paul's words:

> Anyone who speaks in a tongue does not speak to people but to God. Indeed, no one understands them; they utter mysteries by the Spirit. But the one who prophesies speaks to people for their strengthening, encouraging and comfort. Anyone who speaks in a tongue edifies themselves, but the one who prophesies edifies the church. I would like every one of you to speak in tongues, but I would rather have you prophesy. The one who prophesies is greater than the one who speaks in tongues, unless someone interprets, so that the church may be edified ...
>
> For this reason the one who speaks in a tongue should pray that they may interpret what they say. For if I pray in a tongue, my spirit prays, but my mind is unfruitful. So what shall I do? I will pray with my spirit, but I will also pray with my understanding; I will sing with

my spirit, but I will also sing with my understanding. Otherwise when you are praising God
in the Spirit, how can someone else, who is now
put in the position of an inquirer, say "Amen"
to your thanksgiving, since they do not know
what you are saying? You are giving thanks well
enough, but no one else is edified.

I thank God that I speak in tongues more
than all of you. But in the church I would rather
speak five intelligible words to instruct others
than ten thousand words in a tongue.

1 Corinthians 14:2–5, 13–19

In this passage, Paul directly addresses some very
important questions:

What is speaking in tongues?

Many people think that speaking in tongues is an
out of control, ecstatic utterance where a person loses
control of their mouth. Weird stuff. But that's not at
all what Paul describes. The Greek word Paul uses—
most often translated as "tongues"—literally means
"languages" and probably should have been translated
that way initially. To talk about "speaking in languages"
doesn't feel nearly as weird.

Paul also states that these languages are not known
by the person praying. In 1 Corinthians 14:15, he
describes this experience as "pray[ing] with my spirit."
Speaking in tongues is a spirit to Spirit form of communication that, in a sense, bypasses the mind. The person
praying in tongues doesn't understand what they are
praying, unless God gives them a specific interpretation.

One other important truth to notice is that speaking
in tongues is a form of prayer to God. Paul says in
verse 2, "For anyone who speaks in a tongue does not

speak to people but to God." He also states in verse 16, "When you are praising God in the Spirit ..." When someone speaks in tongues, they are offering prayers or praise directly to God, doing so in a language they don't understand. It involves our spirit communicating with the Holy Spirit. From Paul's description, we discover the following definition:

> *Speaking in tongues is prayer or praise spoken to God in a language the speaker does not understand.*[2]

Why is speaking in tongues given by God?

What is the purpose of this particular manifestation of the Spirit? Many people dismiss tongues altogether simply because the practice seems weird and makes no sense to them. But Paul doesn't go there. Even though he's writing to a church that is abusing this gift by making it a requirement for maturity, Paul refuses to dismiss tongues as unimportant.

Instead, he strikes a wonderful balance. The key to living in this balance is to understand the purpose of tongues. Paul describes two *Paul refuses to dismiss tongues as unimportant.* different expressions of tongues—the *public* expression of tongues and the *private* expression of tongues. Each has a very different purpose.

When discussing the public expression of tongues, Paul encourages the church to use the gift of prophecy instead. "But in the church I would rather speak five intelligible words to instruct others than ten thousand words in a tongue" (1 Corinthians 14:19). Paul is responding to a specific situation where people simultaneously spoke in tongues during a worship service, resulting in distraction and disorder. Wisely, Paul urges them to focus instead on the gift of prophecy when the church is gathered. After all, prophecy is directed to the church; tongues is directed to God.

Paul doesn't completely dismiss the public use of tongues, but he does give some fairly strict guidelines. Tongues spoken in a worship service must be expressed decently and in order—one person at a time and with an interpretation (see verses 27, 40). Paul's main concern is the potential for confusion, which explains why he downplays its use in public services and encourages prophecy instead.

In the church I pastor, we choose to apply this principle by not allowing a person to come up front in a worship service and speak out loud in tongues. Our concern is not with the validity of the gift, but rather the increased potential for confusion, since we don't know everyone who may be in attendance. For churches that allow public tongues, Paul's call for order and an interpretation should guide the practice.

Clearly, Paul valued speaking in tongues when used in a private setting, as a personal prayer language.

Now some read Paul's words and conclude that he felt negatively about speaking in tongues. Nothing could be further from the truth. Clearly, Paul valued speaking in tongues *when used in a private setting, as a personal prayer language.* That's what makes all the difference. This explains why Paul says in verses 18-19, "I thank God that I speak in tongues more than all of you. But in the church I would rather speak five intelligible words to instruct others than ten thousand words in a tongue."

Paul thanks God that he speaks in tongues ... more than any of them. He obviously enjoyed speaking in tongues as part of his prayer life. In fact, he states in verse 4, "Anyone who speaks in a tongue edifies themselves, but the one who prophesies edifies the church."

I have heard people use this Scripture to argue against speaking in tongues. "Paul says that tongues only edifies yourself. How self-centered and unhealthy." But that's not Paul's argument. He doesn't criticize tongues or cast it in a negative light. In fact, notice what he says next: "I would like every one of you to speak in tongues, but I would rather have you prophesy ... so that the church may be edified" (1 Corinthians 14:5).

Paul utilizes the genius of the both/and rather than an either/or. His point is not, *Prophecy is good, speaking in tongues is bad.* No. Paul is saying, *"In the church, prophecy is better because it edifies the church. But in private, I love speaking in tongues because it edifies my soul and benefits my relationship with God. I wish all of you spoke in tongues in your personal prayer life because of how edifying this can be to you personally."*

Tongues in a private setting has great value and purpose, wonderfully enhancing a person's prayer life. Are you ever unsure of what to pray? Tongues can be a great way to pray in that situation, letting the Spirit pray through you. If you look down on those who speak in tongues, I urge you to reconsider your response in light of Paul's words. Paul clearly enjoyed and benefitted from speaking in tongues in his prayer life, and he hoped others would experience this as well.

Should everyone speak in tongues?

This question has caused significant conflict and tension throughout the history of Christianity. Had people simply embraced Paul's balance, there wouldn't have been a problem. Instead, many who experienced tongues began to make it a requirement for spiritual maturity or an indicator of Spirit fullness. Because the experience was so wonderful for them, they determined that everyone *should* speak in tongues. And those who didn't felt less spiritual and less mature.

Is that Paul's perspective? Clearly not. In 1 Corinthians 12, Paul argues the case that we all have different gifts and that's what makes the body of Christ so wonderfully diverse. We need each other. He then specifically addresses this topic: "Do all have gifts of healing? Do all speak in tongues? Do all interpret?" (1 Corinthians 12:30). The rhetorical answer is clearly "no." Not everyone has every gift, which means not everyone will have the gift of tongues.

Paul then goes on to say in the next verse: "And yet I will show you the most excellent way. If I speak in the tongues of men or of angels, but do not have love, I am only a resounding gong or a clanging symbol" (1 Corinthians 12:31–13:1). No matter what gift is being exercised, love is the most important factor. It is not loving to exalt the gift of tongues in such a way that two Christian camps are formed: the "haves" and "have nots". We are one in Christ and there are different gifts.

Now having said that, I don't want to swing the pendulum too far this direction without reminding us of Paul's words in 1 Corinthians 14:5, "I would like every one of you to speak in tongues." Paul wanted every one of them to enjoy a prayer language. So how do we put this together? Simple. We shouldn't use tongues as a requirement or measurement of spirituality, and yet at the same time, we should acknowledge the value of tongues in people's prayer lives, encouraging them to ask God for this gift if they want it. That's the balance Paul strikes in this passage. I love this balance because it means we can relax about this gift!

If you have it, great. Use it in your personal prayer times. God gave you this gift to help edify your prayer life. Don't neglect it. Use it.

If you don't have it and don't want it, that's fine. Don't worry about it. No big deal. You're not any less Spirit-filled. Relax.

That of course leaves one more option: What if you don't have it but you think you may want it? After hearing this gift described in this chapter, perhaps you would like this in your prayer life. What should you do?

My Own Story

Perhaps my own story might be helpful in this regard. I have already shared about how in college some friends told me that if I didn't speak in tongues, I wasn't baptized in the Spirit or filled with the Spirit. That caused me to study Scripture. As a result, I became convinced that the Bible did not teach what they were saying. I *could* be filled with the Spirit without speaking in tongues.

For the next few years after college, I felt a bit skittish about this tongues thing. However, at some point God began to stir in my heart a deeper longing for Him, a desire to experience His Spirit more deeply. I found my heart more open and hungry for God's Spirit to heal, to speak, and to move in powerful ways beyond my limited experience.

For the first time ever, I began asking God for this gift—not out of any requirement for spirituality but rather out of a hunger for more of Him. I read books on this subject and listened to pastors like Jack Hayford and John Wimber, who presented a balanced and yet open perspective on this topic. For years, I asked God to give me this gift. I kept on asking, but to no avail. At times I became quite frustrated at God. Why not me?

I now see the wisdom of God's timing but I certainly didn't at that time[3].

Sometime later, some friends from out of town visited my wife and me. In the course of the conversation, we mentioned our desire to receive this gift. They offered to pray for us and we readily agreed. Laying their hands on us, they prayed a simple prayer, asking that we might receive the gift of tongues. Sure enough, Raylene started speaking in a prayer language—but nothing was happening to me. My initial thought was, *Here I go again; someone else is going to get this and not me.*

They kept praying and very soon, I began to feel a syllable just waiting to come out of my mouth. So I began to whisper (I was too embarrassed to do this out loud) and sure enough, that syllable turned into more syllables. I had a prayer language. It wasn't a huge amount—just a short phrase that repeated—but it was a start. Since then, that phrase has grown larger. I now often use this prayer language when praying alone or quietly when praying for others.

For my wife, Raylene, this gift from God was and continues to be a huge blessing. Her prayer life accelerated when she received this gift, and she hasn't looked back. What a wonderful blessing this gift is in our lives. I thank God we have a prayer language. I'm not saying everyone has to have one. I'm just sharing our own story.

Let's Talk About Some Practical Matters

From our experience, we learned a few practical insights about receiving this gift. One, this gift is often received by having someone with the gift pray for you. A few friends of mine received this gift when they were by themselves, but the vast majority received it through the laying on of hands.

Secondly, this gift does not manifest itself apart from our will. Up to that point, my wife and I thought that when or if we ever received this gift, it would take control of our tongue, making us babble uncontrollably. We discovered this isn't how speaking in tongues works. Paul explains later in 1 Corinthians 14 that people who have this gift can start or stop speaking in tongues at any moment in time. They control it (see 1 Corinthians 14:27–28).

Here's the practical application: If God wants to give you this gift, there will come a moment when—in order to receive it—you must consciously begin speaking. God is not going to speak for you, taking control of your mouth, and supernaturally causing words to come forth. You will have to take that first step and speak whatever syllable is on your tongue. For me, the sensation was that of having the beginning of a syllable waiting on my lips. When I started to speak that syllable, more was given. So if you are at that point, take that first step and then see what happens.

Please hear me: I am not talking about someone coaching you on what to say, giving you specific syllables. "Repeat after me … 'Shoulda bought a Honda, shoulda bought a Honda …'" Let's not go there (although I do love Hondas). Speaking in tongues is not man-made nor is it something we should force or copy. If God gives you this gift, it will be unique to you.

Sometimes people worry about the possibility of being deceived. "How do we know this is from God? What if it's of the devil?" In answer to that question, we do what Jesus told us to do: look at the fruit. Is there any reason why the devil would want my wife's prayer life to improve? Is there any reason he would want to give her something that would cause her intimacy with Jesus to grow? I don't think so. There's no need to be afraid of this. If you receive it and are concerned about whether or not it's from God, just look at the fruit. Does it draw you closer to God? Does it help you pray?

I once spoke with a young woman who had received this gift but was concerned it might not be from God. I showed her Paul's words in 1 Corinthians 12:3 where he provides a practical test to determine this. "No one who is speaking by the Spirit of God says 'Jesus be cursed,' and no one can say, 'Jesus is Lord,' except by the Holy Spirit." So I asked her to begin praying quietly in tongues, and then I asked her if she could declare Jesus as Lord. She did. Immediately her heart was at peace about using this gift.

You Can Relax About It

After having this gift for about ten years, I recently "came out of the closet" during a sermon on this subject and told my congregation my story. I had waited so long for fear of being labeled or misunderstood. My fear was unfounded. People appreciated hearing about the subject, since it is rarely discussed. Some, who had always viewed tongues-speaking as weird and of no benefit, thanked me for helping them see the value of this practice. Others had received the gift long ago but didn't know what to do with it. Some had never told anyone in the church for fear of being ostracized or labeled. They too thanked me for affirming something God had given to them.

As far as I know, no one got mad or left the church. We really can relax about this topic. Speaking in tongues is a private and beautiful gift God may want to give some of you. If He does, enjoy it … but don't make a big deal out of it. Certainly don't push it onto others. Just relax in this gift.

- If you have it, enjoy it as a blessing from God.
- If you want it, ask for it.
- If you don't want it, that's fine.
- If you've asked for it and not received it, trust God with this, and then use the other gifts He has given you.

It's all good. The most important lesson to remember is this: *The Spirit longs to help us in our praying.* He intercedes for us when we don't know what to pray. He prompts us to pray for things that are on the Father's heart. And at times, He gives us the gift of tongues to help us grow in our experience of prayer. Don't go it alone in your prayer life. Let the wind of the Spirit fill and empower your praying. This may at times feel a bit uncomfortable, but you'll never regret it.

Section Four

Experiencing the Spirit's Fullness

Chapter Eleven

Are You Spirit-Filled?

—⧄—

"Have you been baptized in the Spirit?"
"Are you Spirit-filled?"

In college, well-meaning friends asked me these questions, and I struggled to answer them. Was I missing something? Christians use these terms "baptism in the Spirit" and "filled with the Spirit" in a variety of ways, resulting not only in confusion but also frustration as lines get drawn in the sand regarding who's "in" and who's "out."

In response, some choose to ignore this topic altogether and keep a polite distance from the Spirit. But that only leads to a lifeless relationship with the Spirit, rather than the vital experience to which these phrases point. Is there another option?

Let's take a fresh look at how the New Testament uses these terms. In doing so, we will discover that, rather than bringing division and confusion, they open the door to a deeper experience of the Spirit available to every believer, including you.

What Does "Baptism in the Spirit" Really Mean?

In Acts 1:4–5, Jesus declares: "Do not leave Jerusalem, but wait for the gift my Father promised, which you have heard me speak about. For John baptized with water, but in a few days you will be baptized with the Holy Spirit." We learn a great deal from these verses.

Jesus describes the baptism of the Spirit as "the gift my Father promised." To what promise is He referring? We discover the answer in the next chapter of Acts. After the Spirit came in power, Peter stood before the curious crowd and explained what had just happened. Interestingly, he quotes an Old Testament promise from the book of Joel.

> And afterward, I will pour out my Spirit on all people. Your sons and daughters will prophesy, your old men will dream dreams, your young men will see visions. Even on my servants, both men and women, I will pour out my Spirit in those days.   Joel 2:28–29

This reveals a radical difference from how people had experienced the Holy Spirit. In the Old Testament, the Spirit was only given to certain people for particular tasks. But this promise declares that one day, God will pour out His Spirit on *all* His people — men, women, sons, daughters, servants, young, old. Everyone gets in on the action.

Clearly Jesus' phrase "baptized with the Holy Spirit" refers to that moment when something dramatic and new happens — the Spirit of God actually comes to permanently reside within His people forever. Rather than the indwelling presence of the Spirit being a possibility, as in the Old Testament, it now becomes an internal reality.

So *when* does this baptism occur? The text is clear. Look at Peter's explanation to the questioning crowd in Acts 2: "Repent and be baptized, every one of you, in the name of Jesus Christ for the forgiveness of your sins. And you will receive the gift of the Holy Spirit. The promise is for you and your children" (Acts 2:38–39).

Notice how Peter uses the same language as Jesus in Acts chapter 1: the "gift" and the "promise". Both Jesus and Peter understood what would happen to these people the moment they repented and placed their faith in Christ. They would be baptized in the Spirit, i.e. the Spirit would come to live in them.

Paul uses similar language in 1 Corinthians 12:13 to describe this amazing reality. "For we were all baptized by [or "in" in the Greek] one Spirit so as to form one body — whether Jews or Gentiles, slave or free — and we were all given the one Spirit to drink." When we place our trust in Jesus and receive the salvation He offers, at that moment He baptizes us in the Spirit.

When we place our trust in Jesus and receive the salvation He offers, at that moment He baptizes us in the Spirit.

The very Spirit of God comes to live in us permanently. Incredible. This promise is now for us. If you have placed your trust in Jesus, the very Spirit of God lives in you. You have been baptized in the Spirit!

It's worth mentioning two passages in Acts that are often used to defend the idea that baptism in the Spirit happens *after* conversion. Both describe unique circumstances regarding the ministry of the Spirit. One occurs in Acts 8:12–17 where Philip, who is not an apostle, ministers in Samaria. There, a group of Samaritans receive Jesus, but not the Spirit. Later, Peter and John are sent by the other apostles to check out what occurred. When they pray for these new believers, they immediately receive the Spirit. Why the delay in receiving the Spirit?

One plausible explanation for the delay until the apostles arrived is that these conversions occurred in Samaria. In that day, Samaritans and Jews did not get along. Given the potential for conflict or misunderstanding regarding this expansion of the gospel, God chose to withhold the giving of the Spirit until the apostles arrived and confirmed God's activity, thus protecting the unity of the church in those crucial early days. When an Ethiopian came to Christ under the ministry of Philip later in that same chapter, the apostles were *not* sent to confirm this conversion. The uniqueness of the Samaritan situation necessitated a unique apostolic response.

Also, the text declares that when Peter and John placed their hands on them, the Samaritans "received the Holy Spirit" (Acts 8:17). The word "received" speaks of someone's initial experience of the Spirit at conversion.

The second passage, Acts 19:1-7, describes Paul meeting some disciples in Ephesus. When he prayed for them, they received the Spirit in a dramatic way. While this initially appears to indicate a baptism of the Spirit occurring after conversion, the text explains that these people were disciples of John, but didn't even know about Jesus. Clearly, they are not yet Christians. So when they received Jesus, they were baptized in the Spirit at that moment.

You Can Experience More Than Baptism

So if the baptism of the Spirit occurs when we place our trust in Christ, what word describes the Spirit's activity in our lives *after* our conversion? The New Testament most often uses the word "filled." We are urged to be filled with the Spirit. This word speaks of more than simply the indwelling presence of the Spirit in us. "Filling" describes a supernatural empowering for life and ministry.

So what does it mean to be filled with the Spirit? Great question ... but not easy to answer. Most people don't realize that two different Greek words are translated "fill" in the New Testament, and each has a different meaning.

One is the Greek work *plero-o*; the other is the word *pimplemi*. To experience the filling of the Spirit, we must understand both of them. In what remains of this chapter, we will focus on the first of these two words, leaving the second word for the next chapter.

> *To be filled with the Spirit involves allowing the Holy Spirit to permeate your thinking, your emotions, your attitudes, and your heart.*

In Ephesians 5:18 Paul writes, "Do not get drunk on wine, which leads to debauchery. Instead be filled with the Spirit." Here Paul uses the word *plero-o*, which refers to *a continual, inner working of the Spirit within us.* The negative analogy of drunkenness confirms this personal, inward experience of the Spirit. When a person is drunk, alcohol exerts a powerful influence in their entire body, impacting them physically, emotionally, and cognitively. In a similar (and yet positive) way, the Spirit can exert significant influence in our entire being. To be filled with the Spirit involves allowing the Holy Spirit to permeate your thinking, your emotions, your attitudes, and your heart. Every part of you filled with the Spirit.

John gives us a vivid and instructive picture of the meaning of this word *plero-o* in chapter 12 of his gospel account. Just days before Jesus was crucified, He visited the home of his friends Lazarus, Mary, and Martha.

Here a dinner was given in Jesus' honor. Martha served, while Lazarus was among those reclining at the table with him. Then Mary took about a pint of pure nard, an expensive perfume; she poured it on Jesus' feet and wiped his feet with her hair. And the house was filled with the fragrance of the perfume.   John 12:2–3

What a powerful scene. Mary expresses her love to Jesus in a beautiful and extravagant way — by anointing His feet with an expensive perfume. John explains that the house was "filled with the fragrance of the perfume." That word "filled" is the word *plero-o*. A fragrance fills a room, not by replacing the air that is there, but rather by permeating it. Wherever you stand, you experience the aroma.

A few years ago I let a friend borrow my car to transport some soup mixes to sell at an arts and crafts fair in a city a few hours away. A few days later, he returned the car in immaculate condition ... except it reeked of chili pepper. Vacuuming didn't help. Neither did leaving the windows open at night. That fragrance permeated my car for weeks. That's *plero-o*. The Spirit wants to permeate every facet of our lives, continually filling us with His fragrance, His peace, His power, His wisdom, His life.

Not surprisingly, Luke uses this word in the book of Acts to describe the Spirit's internal, transformational ministry in a person's life. When needing to delegate a ministry responsibility, the apostles directed the church to "Choose seven men from among you who are known to be full (*pleres*, the basic word that *plero-o* comes from) of the Spirit and wisdom" (Acts 6:3). The apostles are describing someone whose life exudes the fragrance and influence of the Spirit (see Acts 7:55 for another example).

How Does This Filling Happen?

This incredible reality can be ours—to be so permeated by the Spirit of God that our lives are transformed. We increasingly experience the fruit of the Spirit described in Galatians 5:22. "But the fruit of the Spirit is love, joy, peace, forbearance, kindness, goodness, faithfulness, gentleness, and self control." Don't we all long to experience these qualities more consistently? Absolutely! So how does this happen? How can we be filled in this way?

In Ephesians 5:18, Paul gives some specific clues about how we can experience this ongoing filling of the Spirit. This is no formula, mind you. The Spirit doesn't operate according to our formulas. But we can help facilitate in our souls an atmosphere that is more conducive to His activity.

The foundational heart posture required for us to experience the continual filling of the Spirit is *surrender*—surrendering our lives to Jesus' lordship and influence. Notice, Paul doesn't say "fill yourself" with the Spirit. That would be a verb in active voice: *You* go do this. Paul instead uses passive voice. Be filled. The Spirit is the one who fills. He is the primary agent, the activator.

So if the Spirit is the primary activator, what are we supposed to do? We *allow* Him to do what He wants. That's what Paul's "be filled" command means. Welcome the Spirit's fragrance and influence to permeate every area of your life. Often when I'm on my way to meet with someone, I offer a quick prayer, asking the Spirit to fill me and guide me in the conversation. Sometimes in the midst of a tense conversation with a person, I silently utter a "Holy

Welcome the Spirit's fragrance and influence to permeate every area of your life.

Spirit, help me" prayer. As discussed in chapter two, the Spirit waits to be wanted. We can ask Him to fill us any time, day or night.

In a very real sense, we are the gatekeepers on this. The Spirit stands ready and able to fill every part of us, but we guard the gate. We say "yes" or "no" to His activity. So what keeps us from doing this more often?

Here's an analogy I find helpful. Think of your life as a house. Each room represents a different facet: the living room represents your friendships, the office is where you work on finances or your vocation. In the recreation room, you enjoy various leisure activities, while the bedroom represents your intimate and private activities. And everyone has that basement closet in which to store various items from the past. All of these areas and more make up our lives. In order to be filled with the Spirit, we must allow the Holy Spirit into every room in our house. But this is not how we usually live, is it?

Is the Spirit simply resident in our lives or is He president?

What we typically do, consciously or subconsciously, is say to the Spirit, *"Okay, you can be in the living room where our small group meets and around the dinner table where our family discusses things. But I don't really want you hanging around my bedroom, where my girlfriend and I sleep together or where I surf the web. Please stay away from my office area where I do my finances. And I certainly don't want you near that secret locked closet downstairs where I keep those things from my past that I'm ashamed of. So if you could just kind of stay in the living room and kitchen of my house, that would be great."* We're grateful the Spirit lives in our home, but we make sure He doesn't have full access to our lives and hearts. No wonder we don't experience the transformation we desire.

When I was in seminary, a group of my friends gathered on certain evenings to pray. Sometimes an older pastor from India joined us. Thomas was a wonderful, gentle man; a man I would describe as being full of the Spirit. I will never forget a phrase he regularly prayed in his deep, Indian accent: "Spirit, I ask you to not simply be resident but president." That simple phrase describes what makes the difference between a cordial relationship with the Spirit and one that is life-giving and transformative. Is the Spirit simply resident in our lives, or is He president?

The Holy Spirit longs to permeate every area of our lives with the fragrance of His grace and power, His joy and peace. What would that look like for you? What area in your life has a DO NOT ENTER sign posted on the door? Maybe it's ...

- Your finances—You've made it clear you are in control of how much you spend or give.
- Your sexuality—You love Jesus but don't want the Spirit influencing your thought life or the activities in which you engage.
- Your relationships—You continue to harbor bitterness toward someone who hurt you.
- Your work—You choose to compromise your integrity in order to make a sale.
- Your past—You've locked in a closet some shameful secret in your past.

Here's the good news: No matter what your fear, no matter what garbage lies behind that door, the Spirit longs to bring the presence of Jesus into that place. He wants to fill you with all that has already been purchased for you on the cross: His incredible love and forgiveness, His immeasurable mercy and grace, His transformative power and life. The Spirit waits for you to open those doors. Will you allow Him in? This surrender can happen in a moment's notice:

- Rather than bursting out in anger toward your child who just disobeyed again, you can stop at that moment and turn your heart toward Jesus, asking the Spirit to fill you.
- Rather than allowing jealousy to take root in your heart toward another person who is more successful than you, you can stop and welcome the love of the Spirit to fill your heart, reminding you that you are loved and accepted in Christ.
- Rather than hurrying from meeting to meeting throughout your day, you can stop momentarily and welcome the Spirit's presence into the next conversation.

The Holy Spirit longs to bring His influence into our everyday situations and frustrations. Will we allow Him to do that?

HOLY SPIRIT LABORATORY

Take a moment right now and ask the Lord to reveal any DO NOT DISTURB signs that you have posted over certain areas of your life. In what areas are you not allowing the Spirit to influence? And why? Don't move past this question too quickly. Why are you keeping Him out of those places? Is it a fear of letting go? Is it shame? Is it love for the sin?

> Now, are you willing to welcome the Spirit's presence into those areas? Remember, He loves you and already knows about those things. When your heart is ready, ask the Holy Spirit to fill each of those areas of your life.
>
> What would it look like for you to regularly offer this prayer to Him, allowing Him to continually transform you in that area?

You Can't Experience the Spirit Alone

In addition to the importance of surrender, Paul describes in Ephesians 5:18–19 another critical and yet easily ignored facet of experiencing Spirit fullness. "Be filled with the Spirit, speaking to one another ..." We easily forget that this command is written not simply to individuals, but to the church as a whole. The filling of the Spirit happens in *community*, when we speak the truth in love to one another or when we share honestly about our brokenness.

A real relationship with the Spirit involves real relationships with others. We can't be filled with the Spirit on our own.

We all instinctively know that sin thrives in secret. In the darkness of isolation our sins exert their greatest power. Over the years I've seen numerous people who, when their secret sin is finally discovered, experience deep relief. The power of the sin dissipates once it's brought into the light. Of course, everything within us resists acknowledging our sin for fear of rejection or feelings of shame. But once we drag our sin into the light, we often discover the incredible power of grace-filled community.

I know a number of men who struggle with pornography. In the midst of the battle, everything within us wants to keep this struggle a secret. We feel afraid, ashamed, and overwhelmed by our powerlessness. One day, a friend of mine decided to open up to his wife about his secret struggle. Though the conversation was painful, she extended grace in a beautiful way.

Immediately, my friend sensed the Spirit filling those dark places, lifting off of him the stranglehold of the sin. In the midst of his ongoing battle, he discovered a vital spiritual principle: A real relationship with the Spirit involves real relationships with others. We can't be filled with the Spirit on our own.

Do you want to be filled with the Spirit? If so, let me ask: Are you in authentic relationships with other believers? Do you have a few friendships in which you withhold no secrets? Are there people in your life who truly know you, including the weaknesses you have and the sins you struggle with? Without that kind of authentic community, we miss a huge part of what we need to experience Spirit fullness.

Praise Activates the Spirit's Power

Paul mentions one more essential element for being filled with the Spirit. Look again at Ephesians 5:18–20:

> Instead, be filled with the Spirit, speaking to one another with psalms, hymns, and songs from the Spirit. Sing and make music from your heart to the Lord, always giving thanks to God the Father for everything in the name of our Lord Jesus Christ.

Notice the connection between worship and the activity of the Spirit. When we offer our heartfelt worship to God, we open the door for the Spirit to move in us in ways He otherwise would not.

Returning to the house analogy I used earlier, worship is like opening the windows of our house to let in the fresh air. In our home, we installed an attic fan, which we absolutely love to use during the summers. Because temperatures in Colorado cool down significantly in the evenings, we open our windows at night and turn the fan on. As it pulls air from our house into the

Worship is like opening the windows on a cool, summer evening.

attic, it also pulls outside air into our home. We determine which room gets fresh, cool air by simply opening the window of that room.

Worship is like opening the windows on a cool, summer evening. Life's circumstances may get hot and stuffy. We may experience stress at work or at home or school, or perhaps we're enmeshed in a challenging relationship. In the midst of all that, how do we open the windows and let the presence of the Spirit in? Paul tells us: choose to worship Jesus from your heart. Paul specifically encourages several worshipping activities: psalms, hymns, songs from the Spirit, and thanksgiving. Let's look at each.

Psalms

"Psalms" refers to using Scriptures that declare God's praise. Have you ever wanted to praise God but haven't really known what to say? In your Bible, you have an entire book focused on praise. The 150 chapters of the book of Psalms provide practical help in learning how to express praise to God. The psalms function like a greeting card. Sometimes we purchase a greeting card that has no words in it so we can compose our own thoughts. But more often than not, we choose a card that already has words, words that articulate what we want to say.

The psalms can help us articulate praise to God throughout our day. You can arrive early at your office and read some psalms aloud, or perhaps do so with your family immediately after dinner. By intentionally offering praise, we open the windows and allow the Spirit's presence to fill us.

Hymns

"Hymns" most likely refer to prewritten songs—songs written for worship. How engaged are we in worshipping the Lord through singing at church? Do we sing without thinking about the words, or do we fully engage in worship to the Lord? And what about when we're not in church? Think of the moments in your day where opportunities exist to engage in heartfelt worship—while driving in the car, exercising, or as part of your quiet time with God. "Sing and make music from your heart to the Lord" (Ephesians 5:19).

Songs from the Spirit

"Songs from the Spirit" (verse 19) probably refers to spontaneous songs of praise that well up within us, where we make up the lyrics as we praise God. This may be a new experience for you, but why not try it sometime? While in the shower or alone in the car or during a time alone with God, sing a new song to Him. Sing to God the praise that is on your heart.

Giving thanks

Paul then says in verse 20 " … always giving thanks to God the Father for everything, in the name of our

Lord Jesus Christ." Scripture repeatedly urges us to be thankful (for example, Psalm 100:4, 1 Thessalonians 5:18, Colossians 3:15). In the book of Numbers, we see numerous examples of what happens when God's people turn to griping and complaining rather than thanksgiving (see Numbers 11:1-3, 14:1). Not only does ungratefulness darken our outlook; it also closes the window to the fresh breath of God's Spirit into our hearts and our circumstances.

In her book, *One Thousand Gifts*, Ann Voskamp describes the power of seeing and thanking God for every gift that comes our way. She was challenged by a friend to list one thousand things that she loved. Look at the result:

> I took the dare, accepted the challenge, kept track of one thousand things, one thousand gifts—a thousand *graces*—on a quiet, unassuming blog. Before I knew it, thankfulness to God began to fully change me.
>
> What I actually found—startling!—was more daily wonder and surprising beauty than I even expected. And in a few short years, this daily hunt for God's grace, His glory, *had* ushered me into a fuller life. A life of joy! … in giving thanks for each moment and savoring it as bread from His hand, I'd find sustenance and the grace of God Himself in it.[1]

A simple decision to choose gratitude opened the window of her heart to a deeper experience of the Spirit's presence. So often we don't notice all the blessings in our lives, all the gifts God has placed before us. We focus only on what is wrong with our circumstances, what is wrong with the people we work with or the person we are married to. When we choose to thank God for every blessing in our lives throughout our day, we open a door for the Spirit to breathe His joy, peace, and life into our hearts. Gratitude doesn't change our circumstances, but it does enable us to respond differently in the power of the Spirit. We experience life differently.

HOLY SPIRIT LABORATORY

Begin a list of gifts God has given you today. Take a moment and thank Him for each item on this list.

God invites you to open up the window of your heart, letting His Spirit move in you through ...

- a heart of surrender
- a decision to open up and share honestly with a close friend
- the expression of praise and thanksgiving in the midst of life's challenges

However it happens, the result will be an increasing influence of the Spirit's presence and activity in your life. *Be filled with the Spirit!*

Chapter Twelve

When the Spirit Comes in Power

—⟋ⱳ⟍—

A few years ago, my wife and I entered into a totally new world — we became parents of a college student. We soon discovered that entering into that world involves learning a new vocabulary. Words I had never heard before suddenly became part of our dinner conversations (can you say "FAFSA"?). Not only that, words I thought I knew the meaning of were redefined right before my eyes.

For instance, I actually thought I knew what the word "award" meant — until we received our first "award" letter from a university. Initially we were thrilled to read that all the costs of attending the school had been "awarded" to my soon-to-be freshman daughter. In the midst of celebrating, I reread the letter and discovered that most of the offer came in the form of loans. They were giving me the "award" of borrowing money. Needless to say, the celebration stopped. We were using the same word, but with a very different meaning.

The Tale of *Plero-o* and *Pimplemi*

A similar confusion occurs when we talk about the ministry of the Holy Spirit. While every Christian acknowledges the importance of being filled with the Spirit, we often fail to realize that two different Greek words in the New Testament are used to describe this experience.

The most commonly understood word is *plero-o*, which, as we saw in the previous chapter, describes the Spirit's permeating presence within, filling every area of our lives (as in Ephesians 5:18). For years I was taught and believed that any New Testament use of the word "fill" as it relates to the Spirit refers to this inward, continuous kind of filling. Imagine my surprise when I learned that another Greek word—also translated "fill"—portrays a different experience with the Spirit.

The Greek word *pimplemi* is often used in Luke and Acts to describe not the internal, ongoing ministry of the Spirit, but rather the Spirit spontaneously "coming upon" someone for a particular task or purpose. For instance, in Luke 1:67 we read that Zechariah "was filled [*pimplemi*] with the Holy Spirit and prophesied." The Spirit spontaneously came upon Zechariah, and he spoke a prophetic word about his newly born son.

A similar experience occurs in Acts 2:4. "All of them were filled [*pimplemi*] with the Holy Spirit and began to speak in other tongues as the Spirit enabled them." This "filling" involved the Spirit spontaneously empowering these believers for a particular ministry opportunity; namely, speaking in tongues, which caused the crowd to gather and express spiritual curiosity.

So what was the nature of this empowering? Was this "filling" a one-time experience so that from that moment on they were "filled" in this way? Apparently not. Just two chapters later in Acts 4, these same believers were gathered for prayer and guess what happens? "After they prayed, the place where they were meeting was shaken. And they were all filled [*pimplemi*] with the Holy Spirit and spoke the word of God boldly" (verse 31). Those filled in chapter 2 were now filled again.

The use of *pimplemi* emphasizes a temporary rather than permanent empowering. These believers experienced the manifest presence of the Spirit in that moment, resulting in the room shaking as well as a supernatural empowering to speak the word of God boldly (see also Acts 13:9).

So what exactly does this mean for us? Sometimes the Spirit chooses to spontaneously manifest His presence in our lives. In other words, we at times may actually experience His presence in a tangible way. These manifestations may be as simple as sensing the Spirit's presence in a room, or as dramatic as an experience I had a number of years ago during a difficult season in my life.

> *Sometimes the Spirit chooses to spontaneously manifest His presence in our lives.*

At the time, our church was growing and people's lives were being impacted. Plans were underway to add a second service, and I was eager to move forward ... until one night when I experienced my first panic attack. Out of the blue, I felt a cold sweat and a racing heartbeat. I didn't know what was happening to me, but the attacks became more frequent. Terrified that I might be losing my mind, I drove several hours to spend some time with a counselor in another city.

During our first session, he skillfully exposed my addiction to performance/church growth[1]. Afterward, I returned to my room to relax and process our conversation from that morning. At one point, I knelt beside the bed and listened to worship music. I wasn't feeling anything in particular or looking for God to do anything miraculous. I just wanted to spend time in His presence.

Soon a song played that spoke about God's love, and suddenly the Spirit of God came upon me in a very real way. I don't know how to describe this other than to say that I experienced tangible waves of joy and love washing over me. What felt like electricity coursed through my body. Such joy welled up within me that I began laughing for several minutes. After it eventually subsided, I didn't know exactly what had happened. But I felt certain the Spirit of God had come upon me, filling me with His presence. What's most amazing to me is that I haven't experienced a panic attack since.

When the Spirit of the living God chooses to manifest His presence, shouldn't we expect that dramatic things might occur?

Probably out of concern of being labeled a "weirdo" and out of reverence for what happened, I haven't shared this experience with many people. But it did happen. This example reminds me that the Spirit may choose to move in ways beyond our comfort zone and yet that benefit us in a deeply spiritual way. Are we open to that possibility?

When the Spirit of the living God chooses to manifest His presence, shouldn't we expect that dramatic things might occur? After all, He is God. The Bible tells us what can happen when the Spirit shows up: John fell over as if dead (Revelation 1:17); the people in Nehemiah 8 began weeping; the believers in Acts 2 were thought to be drunk. In 1 Corinthians 12:7–11, Paul spoke of "manifestations of the Spirit" that included healing and other miracles. These kinds of manifestations should not surprise us, if indeed we believe that God is the holy, powerful, awesome God of the universe.

While these examples are fairly dramatic, the Spirit's manifest presence may also include more gentle — but just as real — phenomena. I have seen people in the midst of profound grief experience the supernatural peace of God descend upon them in a tangible way. Sometimes when the Spirit manifests His presence in a worship service, I feel a tingling sensation in my face. For years I didn't make the connection that this was an indicator of the Spirit's presence. Some people experience warmth in their hands as they pray for healing. All of these are examples of the various ways we may experience the Spirit's manifest presence.

I use the word "various" intentionally. God moves in a variety of ways. Even though these manifestations are powerful when they happen, we shouldn't try to *make* them happen, and we certainly shouldn't use them as a measurement of matu-

The Spirit is like the wind, blowing where He wants, doing what He wants. Our part is to simply be open to the possibility of Him moving in these ways.

rity, looking down on those who haven't had the same experience of the Spirit as us. The Spirit is like the wind, blowing where He wants, doing what He wants. Our part is to simply be open to the possibility of Him moving in these ways. Are we open to that?

You Don't Need to Fear Manifestation Mayhem

I realize that all this talk of manifestations of the Spirit may make some of us a tad nervous. Okay, more than a tad. I understand that. Many of these manifestations fit into the "weird" category — or at least outside of the box. A certain degree of caution is absolutely appropriate. However, I find that many Christians go way beyond cautious in their approach to this topic, closing the door entirely on any tangible manifestations of the Spirit. In doing so, we may be missing ways in which the Spirit longs to move.

Christian history is filled with examples of godly people who experienced the Spirit coming upon them in fairly dramatic ways. In chapter two, I described the experience of D. L. Moody, who, in his own words, "had such an experience of [God's] love that I had to ask Him to stay His hand."[2]

When French philosopher and mathematician Blaise Pascal died, a piece of paper was found sewn into his cloak. On that paper he described an encounter with God that dramatically changed his life on Monday November 23, 1654, "Fire. God of Abraham, God of Isaac, God of Jacob. Not the God of the philosophers and learned. God of Jesus Christ ... Joy, Joy, Joy, tears of joy."[3]

Charles Finney, the great nineteenth-century evangelist, described a personal encounter he experienced with the Spirit: "The Holy Spirit descended upon me in a manner that seemed to go through me, body and soul. I could feel the impression like a wave of electricity, going through and through me. Indeed, it seemed to come in waves and waves of liquid love."[4]

During seasons of revival, these kinds of manifestations of the Holy Spirit were quite common. George Whitefield, whom God used to bring hundreds of thousands to Christ, explained what happened during one of his meetings in 1742:

> Such commotion surely was never heard of, especially at eleven at night. It far outdid all that I ever saw in America. For about an hour and a half

there was such weeping, so many falling into deep distress, and expressing it in various ways ... their cries and agonies were exceedingly affecting.[5]

When Jonathon Edwards, the eighteenth-century pastor, preached his now famous sermon, "Sinners in the Hands of an Angry God," people throughout the congregation wept under the conviction of the Spirit. Those who may want to attribute this to emotional manipulation need to remember that Edwards was a very staid, emotionless preacher who read his sermons in a high-pitched, monotone voice. More likely, the Spirit came upon these people and brought supernatural conviction of sin.

A number of years ago in the midst of my own hungering for more of God's Spirit, I encountered some resistance from a few people in my denomination who felt that God wasn't interested in manifestations like this. In order to better understand our denomination's perspective, I began reading about the history of our movement. Needless to say, I was fascinated to discover the following passage:

It is difficult to describe these tidal-waves of revival. The meetings were charged with intense emotion. Strange scenes were enacted, and strange things happened. Sinners under conviction would come under a peculiar power. They would sometimes fall down as men slain in battle. They would remain that way for a long time, during which intermittent groanings and piercing shrieks would be heard. Then would follow a season of earnest prayer for pardon and mercy.[6]

Even in a denomination not known for its charismatic leanings, our history was influenced by dramatic manifestations in which the Spirit came upon people in tangible ways.

Again let me be clear. I am not advocating for an *emphasis* on these kinds of manifestations, or even assuming they should be normal, everyday experiences. But I want all of us to honestly wrestle with this question: Does our theology include a possibility for this kind of *pimplemi* filling of the Spirit? Are we open to the Spirit of God manifesting His presence in our lives in tangible ways? If not, what might we be missing?

Are These Manifestations From God?

Obviously a very important question arises in this discussion: How can we know if these manifestations come from God? On one hand, we don't want to naively assume that every dramatic manifestation has divine origin. Yet on the other hand, we don't want to categorically reject any such phenomenon simply because it doesn't fit our experience or theological framework. In doing so, we may be missing God's activity. As Martyn Lloyd-Jones declares,

> We must be very careful in these matters. What do we know of the realm of the Spirit? What do we know of the Spirit falling on people? What do we know about these great manifestations of the Holy Spirit? We need to be very careful 'lest we be found fighting against God,' lest we be guilty of 'quenching the Holy Spirit of God.'[7]

He's right. We need to be very careful that we don't categorically dismiss occurrences simply because they seem weird. So how can we avoid this error? How can we accurately assess whether or not a manifestation is from God?

Often our automatic response to this is to ask what seems to be the obvious question: *Is it biblical?* In other words, can we find a passage of Scripture to support this particular manifestation? While I totally understand our desire to ask this question, I have found that it is not as helpful as we might think.

Sometimes people search their Bible concordance for a particular word and then rip verses out of context to prove that what is happening is from God. So for instance, if someone's hands feel hot when they pray, we look for verses about heat or hands. Maybe we find some obscure Old Testament text that mentions hot hands, *Does our theology include a possibility for this kind of filling of the Spirit?* and from that we boldly assert that this manifestation must be biblical. Never mind that the particular passage isn't talking about healing or the Spirit. But because the words we were looking for are mentioned somewhere in the Bible, it must be biblical.

And of course the opposite happens as well. In order to argue that my laughing experience wasn't from God, some may look in Scripture for a similar phenomenon. When no examples are found, the conclusion is drawn: that isn't biblical. However, we do all sorts of things that aren't mentioned in the Bible: teaching from an iPad, projecting words of songs on a video screen, driving to church in a car, using offering envelopes, etc. The list could go on for miles. We all regularly participate in spiritual activities that don't have a Bible verse to describe them. Does that stop us? Of course not.

Rather than asking the "Is it biblical" question, let me suggest two other questions that can help us discern whether or not certain manifestations come from God.

Question #1: Does this violate any teaching or principle from the Bible?

This question gets to the heart of our desire to be biblical and yet doesn't require us to find specific verses for every manifestation. When any manifestation occurs, we can test it with Scripture by asking if it *violates* any principle or command from the Bible. For instance, even though we can't find a particular Bible verse that describes someone's hands feeling hot as they pray for healing, that doesn't mean this is not from God. A better question to ask is, *"Does this violate any teaching of Scripture. Is there any place in the Bible where this experience would be deemed harmful or sinful?"*

Or let's say someone in a worship service feels such a powerful presence of God that they fall over. Does this manifestation violate any principle from Scripture? Initially, we would conclude that it doesn't. No place in Scripture says, "You shall not fall over in a worship service."

Now let's say this same person starts falling over *every* service. We might quickly suspect that this behavior is perhaps more about getting attention than experiencing the Spirit. In that case, a church leader should speak with the person to determine if pride is a factor. While the initial manifestation may have come from God, the subsequent manifestations may be rooted in a need for attention.

This leads to the second question worth asking when discerning whether or not some manifestation comes from God:

Question #2: Does this manifestation bear good fruit?

Jesus urged us to use this criterion when evaluating whether prophets are true or false. Look carefully at what He says:

> Watch out for false prophets. They come to you in sheep's clothing, but inwardly they are ferocious wolves. By their fruit, you will recognize them. Do people pick grapes from thornbushes, or figs from thistles? Likewise every good tree bears good fruit, but a bad tree bears bad fruit...
>
> Not everyone who says to me, "Lord, Lord," will enter the kingdom of heaven, but only the one who does the will of my Father who is in heaven. Many will say to me on that day, "Lord, Lord, did we not prophesy in your name, and in your name drive out demons and perform many miracles?" Then I will tell them plainly, "I never knew you. Away from me, you evildoers."
>
> Matthew 7:15-17, 21–23

Clearly, from Jesus' perspective, we should never automatically assume a powerful manifestation is or isn't from God without looking at the fruit in the person's life and ministry. Are they growing in their maturity, their character, and their love for Jesus? Are others positively impacted by this person's ministry?

Now we must remember that in the natural world, fruit doesn't manifest itself overnight but takes time to develop and reveal its true nature. Similarly, we need to be willing to take time to evaluate these manifestations. Too often, believers automatically and verbally denounce any "outside the box" phenomenon, only later to regret their initial assessment once time reveals its fruitfulness.

During the Great Awakenings, numerous atypical manifestations occurred—people shaking, weeping or falling down under the power of God. Many Christians were troubled by the weirdness of those occurrences. Later on, however, no one could deny the fruit that resulted from those meetings as thousands came to Christ. Jesus' words should cause us to avoid being too hasty in pronouncing that something is of the devil until we have had ample time to evaluate a person's heart and the fruit produced in their lives.

We should never automatically assume a powerful manifestation is or isn't from God without looking at the fruit in the person's life and ministry.

We should not forget Gamaliel's counsel to the Sanhedrin, who eagerly wanted to squash the healing manifestations demonstrated by Peter and John. Gamaliel wisely counseled them, "Let them go! For if their purpose or activity is of human origin, it will fail. But if it is from God, you will not be able to stop these men; you will only find yourselves fighting against God" (Acts 5:38–39). That's good advice. Give it time. Evaluate the fruit before making any hasty decisions one way or the other.

All Ministry Is Messy

While these diagnostic questions can be helpful in discerning whether or not a certain manifestation comes from God, we also need to realize that often ministry involves a mixture of God's activity and our own flesh. A person may experience the Spirit in a profound way, and yet their response might be tainted by their own pride or self-righteousness. This is the reality of our living in a fallen world. My sinful flesh can creep in when I'm teaching a message, as I think to myself, *Wow that point was really good. I bet people are impressed.*

That momentary pride doesn't negate God using my teaching in people's lives. It does, however, remind us that no ministry we engage in, including a dramatic experience of the Spirit, is 100 percent pure and devoid of any sinful flesh. All ministry is messy.

In 1 Corinthians 14, Paul wades into this messiness as it relates to speaking in tongues. As we saw in

When the Spirit moves in powerful and even dramatic ways, church leadership must provide direction to the church regarding how these manifestations will function and in what context.

chapter 10, some who had this gift looked down on those who didn't. Paul didn't respond by declaring that speaking in tongues was not from God. Instead, he articulated some ground rules for the use of this gift in various settings. These ground rules helped mitigate pride and the abuse of the gift.

We learn from his example that when the Spirit moves in powerful and even dramatic ways, church leadership must provide direction to the church regarding how these manifestations will function and in what context. For instance, if a person begins weeping uncontrollably during a service, we might ask one of our prayer team members to take the person into a prayer room. This enables more effective ministry to the person as well as minimizing the potential for significant distraction to others. We want to respond in a way that honors the person and the body of Christ.

I realize other churches may handle this differently—which is perfectly fine. This is not a question of violating Scripture as much as an issue of church leadership deciding how they will approach these matters. At times, I have told our church body, "Hey, if something weird happens in a worship service—like someone falling over or someone beginning to weep uncontrollably—don't freak out and conclude that our church is going off the deep end. Give our church leadership time to assess and evaluate whether or not this is from God and how we believe we as a church should respond."

Are the Windows Open?

The whole of Scripture reminds us that at times the Spirit moves in ways that may seem strange to us, certainly outside of our comfort zone or past experiences. Let's not allow our preconceived boundaries to cause us to miss what He might want to do. A seminary professor of mine used to say regarding these manifestations of the Spirit that he liked to leave the window open but keep the screen on. That's good advice. We can leave the window open for the presence of God to move, and yet also leave the screen on, utilizing prayerful discernment and wise counsel in these matters.

Are you willing to do that? If so, who knows what God might do in your life and your church.

Epilogue

A Simple Prayer for More of the Spirit

—◊—

In this book we have sought to answer one critically important question: How can you experience more of the Spirit in your everyday life? We've learned together how the Spirit can:

- Help you experience greater intimacy with our Heavenly Father
- Enable you to better hear God's voice and be led by Him
- Empower you to pray more effectively for others
- Fill you with His life-changing power

Sounds awesome. So where do we go from here? How do we continue to grow in our experience of the Spirit? The answer is found in a little three-word prayer that I find myself praying throughout the day: *Come Holy Spirit.*

I love that prayer. At times over the years, I have heard some argue that we shouldn't pray this way, since the Spirit already lives within us. Hopefully, since you've made it this far in the book, you realize that while the Spirit lives in us, He desires that we experience more of Him.

We began this journey in chapter 1 with Jesus' amazing statement: "How much more will your Father in heaven give the Holy Spirit to those who ask him?" (Luke 11:13). What an amazing promise … *more* of the Spirit in our lives. Your heart longs for that. Mine too. The Spirit longs for us to experience this as well.

According to Jesus, one specific response is required to see that longing realized: *Asking*. More of the Spirit can be ours *if we ask*. This is not a flippant, half-hearted request but rather an earnest, persistent, even desperate appeal. Why is that so important? In doing so, we demonstrate our need, our dependency, as well as our faith—all of which are fertile soil for God's activity.

Remember, He's not looking for the perfect, the powerful, or those who have their act together. The Spirit does His best work in ordinary people who recognize how desperately they need Him, living every moment of their lives in absolute dependence upon Him.

So whether you are at the grocery store, in your mathematics class, on the tennis court, in a worship service, at your work cubicle, or waking up to begin the day, make this your continual prayer: *Come Holy Spirit*. Regularly invite the Spirit into your everyday life, and then see what happens. Be attentive to His presence and follow His leading. A wonderful adventure awaits you.

Paul gives us a taste of what this adventure might entail:

Now to him who is able to do immeasurably *more* than all we ask or imagine, according to *his power that is at work within us* [He's talking about the Spirit!], to him be glory in the church and in Christ Jesus throughout all generations, for ever and ever! Amen.

Ephesians 3:20–21 (my emphasis)

Sounds exciting. *Come Holy Spirit!*

Additional Resources

How to Help Someone Experience the Spirit's Healing in Their Painful Memories

———※———

Sometimes the pain of the past is significant enough that the Spirit needs to bring healing to a specific memory in order for a person to experience the Father's love. Over the years I have walked many people through a process in which God brings healing to particularly painful memories. I am often astounded at how wonderfully Jesus ministers to a person's painful past.

Here's the process I use when I suspect someone I'm praying with has a memory that hinders their ability to experience the Spirit's love. (Since there is a linear progression to this, I use the term "step" to describe the different aspects. This does not mean this process is a formula. Being led by the Spirit throughout is essential.)

Step One—Wait for a Memory

Ask the Holy Spirit to bring a memory to mind. In this step, we do not tell the person to think of a specific memory.

We simply encourage them to quiet their heart and see if the Lord brings one to mind. It could be from years earlier, or a more recent experience. We trust the Spirit to bring to mind the memory God wants to deal with.

Step Two—Experience the Memory

Ask the person to close their eyes and be "in" the memory. Have them describe what is happening to them. Where are they? Who else is there with them? What is being said/done? What's important here is for the person to actually *feel* the emotions they felt when the event actually happened.

Step Three—Address the Offender

Ask the prayee to address the offending person as if the offender is sitting in front of them, articulating how this person's actions impacted them. For instance, *"Dad, when you yelled at me and told me I was stupid, I felt hurt and ashamed. I felt rejected by you."* Don't hurry this step. They need to fully articulate how this impacted them personally.

Step Four—Extend Forgiveness

When the prayee is ready, have them express aloud forgiveness to the offending party. You may need to explain what forgiveness is and what it isn't.

For instance, *"Forgiveness means to cancel a debt. It does not mean forgetting. It does not mean minimizing the offense or excusing it. Forgiveness says, 'When you did this, it hurt me deeply. But because Jesus has forgiven me on the cross, I choose to let go of my right to retaliate. I bring this offense to the cross.'"*

If they struggle to forgive the offender, ask the Spirit to help them see that person the way their Heavenly Father does.

Step Five—Invite Jesus into the Memory.

You can say something like, *"I'm going to ask Jesus to enter this memory. I want you to let me know when He is there. You may see Him in the room. You may just sense His presence. But let me know when He is there."* Then ask Jesus to come into the memory. Wait until the person senses the presence of Jesus.

Step Six—Renounce Any Sinful Responses

Explain to the prayee that even though this person sinned against them, they may have responded to that offense in a sinful or unhealthy way—by harboring bitterness toward the person, by making vows like, *"I'll never trust a man again,"* or by believing lies, *"I'm a bad person,"* etc. Ask the Holy Spirit to bring to mind any of these responses. With each, have the person bring that to Jesus and verbally confess/renounce it.

Often, we subconsciously project these lies or vows onto our Heavenly Father. *I can't trust God. God could never love me.* Have the person bring to the cross each of these lies/vows that they have subconsciously or consciously held against God.

Step Seven—Ask Jesus to Do Whatever He Wants in the Memory.

Pray a simple prayer: *"Jesus, we invite you to do whatever you want to do in this memory."* Then wait for Him to do that. This is the most powerful part of all, because it allows Jesus to minister directly to the wounded heart.

Don't *suggest* things Jesus might want to do. Simply wait for Him to minister to this person in their memory. After a few minutes, ask the prayee what they experienced Jesus doing. Often they say something like, *"He came over to me and put His arm on my shoulder."* Or *"Jesus stood between me and my abusive father."* Frequently, Jesus will speak to them, affirming His love for them.

Step Eight—Pray for the Person

Pray that God would seal the work He has done in that person, enabling them to live more fully in the reality of the new truth He brought into that painful memory.

I have frequently seen the Spirit of God use this process to bring healing to a painful memory, enabling the person to more deeply experience the Father's love. I realize that for some this process may feel a bit too mystical or even New Age. I encourage you to try it with someone before you jump to that conclusion. This process is rooted in the biblical concepts of forgiving from the heart as well as the Spirit's ministry of bringing healing to the broken-hearted. The entire process is Spirit-led and Jesus-focused.

Study Guide

(For groups or individuals)

—ɯ—

Chapter One: You CAN Experience the Spirit

1. Which of the following words most accurately describes your relationship with the Holy Spirit: distant, intimate, confusing, mysterious, exhilarating, fearful, or something else? Explain.

2. Who or what has made the greatest influence on your current understanding of the Holy Spirit (e.g. pastor, teacher, book, class, etc.)? In what ways did that influence affect you toward the Holy Spirit— either positively or negatively?

3. Has your experience with the Spirit ever been labeled by someone else? If so, what was the label? How did that feel, and how did you respond to the person?

4. What does it mean to you, in practical terms, to experience "fellowship" with the Spirit as described in Philippians 2:1–2 and 2 Corinthians 13:14? What keeps us from experiencing that reality more fully?

5. Read John 14:15–18. List everything Jesus says the Spirit can do in our lives. Which item on that list do you most long to experience more deeply and why?

6. Think of a specific challenge or negative emotion you are experiencing right now. What difference would it make to know that the Spirit of Christ actually lives in you and longs to be invited into this challenge or emotion?

Chapter Two: The Essential, Overlooked Ingredient to More of the Spirit

1. How well do you respond when you have to wait on something? Why is waiting so difficult for most of us?

2. Read Acts 1:4. Why do you think Jesus commanded His disciples to wait for the Spirit?

3. What is the relationship between our weakness and God's Spirit? See 2 Corinthians 12:7–10. Share an example from your life in which personal weakness impacted your experience with the Spirit.

4. When was the last time you stepped out of your comfort zone? How did doing this impact your relationship with God?

5. Read Luke 11:5–13.

    Why are we encouraged to "ask, seek, and knock"?

    What do these verses tell us about the character and nature of God?

    Why does Jesus urge us to pray for the Holy Spirit?

6. How earnestly do you long for more of the Spirit in your life? How significantly does that longing impact your everyday life?

Chapter Three: Loved ... Period

1. While many of us know of Bible verses that talk about God's love, we still struggle to really believe in our hearts that this is true. Why is it so hard for us to believe that God loves us?

2. Read the story of the prodigal son in Luke 15:11–32.

    Which son most struggled to experience the father's love and why?

    Which of the two sons most accurately describes your level of engagement with the Father's love?

3. Look carefully at Romans 8:14–16.

    According to this passage, what causes us to not experience God's love?

What specific things does the Spirit do to help us experience God's love?

How fully have you experienced the "Abba cry"?

How well and how often do you experience the Spirit testifying with your spirit that you are God's child? What might enable you to experience Him and hear His voice more clearly and frequently?

4. Are there wounds in your past that make it hard for you to experience God's love? What might it look like to invite the Spirit of Jesus into those places?

Chapter Four: A Closed Mouth and a Yellow Pad

1   In this chapter, we explored the idea that God wants to speak to us. Does that idea fill your heart with excitement or fear or something else? Why?

2.   Why would God want to speak to you?

3.   List all the examples that come to mind of people in the Bible who heard God speak to them. What stands out to you about this list?

4.   Look at 1 Kings 19:11-13.

What does this passage tell us about how we *expect* God to speak to us and how He may actually do so?

Have you ever experienced the gentle whisper of God? If so, describe the experience. How did you know it was God?

5. What are some ways we can be more attentive to God's gentle whisper?

Chapter Five: Is That Really You, God?

1. We see in the Bible that God speaks in a variety of ways. Why do you think that is?

2. Why is it important that the Bible provides our foundation for hearing God's voice? Why is it important that we not limit God speaking to us only through the Bible?

3. Read Acts 13:2 and Luke 2:27. How do these people hear the Spirit speak? What keeps us from hearing God in these same ways?

4. In Acts 2:17–18, God declares that in this post-Pentecost age of the Spirit, He will speak to His people through visions and dreams. Have you ever experienced God speaking to you through either of these means? Describe.

5. In this chapter, Kraft states, "Many Christians have more faith in the devil's ability to deceive than they do in God's ability to speak." Do you agree or disagree with that statement? Explain.

6. Look again at the four "tests" Kraft offers in discerning whether or not God is speaking. Which of these are most helpful for you as you grow in hearing God's voice?

Chapter Six: Hearing the Spirit for Others

1. What comes to mind when you hear the word "prophecy"?

2. Kraft defines prophecy as "the communication of something God spontaneously brings to our awareness, resulting in a person being strengthened, encouraged, or comforted." How is this definition different than and/or similar to your previous understanding of prophecy?

3. Read 1 Thessalonians 5:20-21. How does this passage impact your attitude and approach toward prophetic words? Explain.

4. Can every Christian prophesy? According to Acts 2:17-18, how would Peter answer that question? According to 1 Corinthians 14:1, how would Paul answer that question?

5. How desirous are you of hearing God speak in this way?

Chapter Seven: How to Share a Prophetic Word … Without Being Weird

1. Have you ever experienced a prophecy "horror story," where someone gave you a word but did so in an unhealthy way? Describe your experience. What would you do differently?

2. Why is it so important that we properly release a prophetic word?

3. Read 1 Corinthians 13. What does this passage tell us about the relationship between love and prophecy? What are some ways prophecy can be released in an unloving manner?

4. Why does prophecy so easily open up a door to pride in our own hearts? How can we maintain humility in exercising this ministry?

5. What are the elements of an effective release of a prophetic word?

6. What is a next step for you to take in your desire to grow in this area?

Chapter Eight: The Spirit of Healing

1. What are your biggest questions or concerns regarding the ministry of healing prayer?

2. Why did Jesus heal the sick? See Matthew 9:35–38 and 14:9–14. What does this tell us about God's heart toward sickness and disease? Why does that matter?

3. Read Luke 9:1–2, 10:1–2, 9 and Acts 6:8. Why does Jesus entrust His healing ministry to others, including those who are not apostles?

4. Kraft states, "The ministry of healing can be a normal part of our experience as Christians." Do you agree or disagree with that statement? Why?

5. Of the two kingdom realities Kraft discussed regarding the "now and the not yet" of the kingdom, which does your life lean towards?

6. How does embracing both of these kingdom realities help us face the question of why not everyone is healed when we pray for them?

Chapter Nine: How to Pray For the Sick

1. Why do we so often hesitate to pray for healing for someone who is sick?

2. Read Matthew 17:14–20 and Mark 6:5–6. What do these passages teach us about the role of faith in healing?

3. What are some dangerous attitudes toward faith in healing that may cause more harm than good? Have you personally experienced any of these? Explain.

4. How would you define faith?

5. What are some observations you can make about how Jesus prayed for the sick? What keeps you from praying that same way?

6. Review the healing prayer model offered in this chapter. If in a small group, spend some time using this model to pray for anyone in your group who has any painful or challenging physical condition. Debrief the experience, from the perspective of those praying as well as those who received prayer.

Chapter Ten: How the Spirit Can Energize Your Prayer Life

1. How satisfying is your experience of prayer?

2. What role does the Spirit play in our prayer lives? See Luke 10:21; Romans 8:14–16, and 26–27.

3. What does it mean to "pray in the Spirit"?

4. Regarding Kraft's discussion of speaking in tongues, what most …

    surprised you?

    confused you?

    challenged you?

5. Where are you at personally as it relates to speaking in tongues, and why?

6. As a group, pray through the Lord's Prayer diagram shown on page 143, taking time for each section. Debrief the experience.

Chapter Eleven: Are You Spirit-Filled?

1. What experiences, thoughts, etc., come to mind when you hear the term "Spirit-filled"?

2. In this chapter, Kraft articulated what the phrase "baptism of the Spirit" refers to. How would you summarize his definition? Do you agree or disagree? Give biblical evidence to support your perspective.

3. Define being "filled with the Spirit" as described by Paul in Ephesians 5:18–19. What role does surrender play in this process?

4. In what specific areas of your life have you posted a Do Not Enter sign as it relates to the ministry and presence of the Spirit? What might it look like to invite Him into those areas?

5. What does it look like to experience the filling of the Spirit in community? If you are in a small group, discuss the level to which you are experiencing this together.

6. What role does giving thanks play in experiencing the Spirit's fullness? How can we be more intentional about this in our everyday lives?

Chapter Twelve: When the Spirit Comes in Power

1. Have you ever had a weird/outside the box experience with the Spirit? If you are comfortable doing so, describe the experience.

2. How would you define the *pimplemi* filling described in this chapter? In what specific ways is this different from the *plero-o* filling described in the previous chapter?

3. Why do we often respond negatively to other people's spiritual manifestations that are outside of our comfort zone or personal experience?

4. What might a more healthy response look like? Read Acts 5:38–39. How might the body of Christ be positively impacted by this response?

5. Are your "windows open" when it comes to the possibility of dramatic manifestations of the Spirit? Why or why not?

6. Spend some time praying for more of the Spirit's presence and power in your life.

Acknowledgements

—∿—

There is no way a project like this could be completed without a team of fantastic people helping make it happen. I want to first of all thank my incredible wife, Raylene, whose patience and grace enabled me to frequently go to the basement office to do some more writing or editing. Thanks also to my incredible children, who continually remind me that I am loved, not because of what I do but just because. Their love inspires me.

Thanks to my church family at Christ Community Church who are journeying with me in the "More" of the Spirit. I'm so grateful for their faith, their love, and their encouragement. Thanks also to my prayer shield (Mike Olearnick, Cindy Chavez, Mark and Martha Hendrickson, Julie Cila, Lynn Stugart, Kathi Polk, Paula Heppner) who prayed this book into being.

I'm so thankful for the number of friends who previewed the manuscript, offering valuable suggestions. These friends include Bob Bever, Arthur Ellison, Jess Mahon, Dr. Tom Kenigsberg, Dr. Wayne Jeffers, Joshua Smith, Rusty Hayes, Bill Shereos, John and Paula Heppner, Lynn Jeffers, Julie Cila, Jeff Foote,

Chris Thompson, Carlos Martinez, Mike Searle, Lynn Stugart, Doug Brown, Bruce Hoppe, and Cindy Chavez.

And finally, a special thanks to Michael J. Klassen and Tom Freiling whose wisdom and expertise helped make this book way better than it ever could have been if working on my own.

Endnotes

—ww—

Chapter One You CAN Experience the Spirit

1. The critical first step in this journey of experiencing the Spirit is to enter into a relationship with God through Christ. Jesus died on the cross to pay the penalty for our sins. We are all sinners, separated from God and deserving of His judgment. But when we place our trust in Jesus, our sins are forgiven and we enter into a love relationship with Him.

    Have you placed your faith in Christ alone for your relationship with God? Are you trusting not in your own effort or goodness, but in what Christ has done on your behalf? If you are not sure, let me suggest some words you can pray to God, communicating your desire to enter into a relationship with Him and thereby receive the Holy Spirit into your life:

    > *Dear God, I long for a relationship with You, but I realize that my sin separates me from that relationship. Thank You for sending Your Son Jesus to die on the cross for my sin. He took upon Himself the penalty I deserved. In this moment, I choose to place my trust in You, Jesus. I ask You to forgive my sin — past, present and future — and to live in me through the presence of Your Spirit.*

> *Change me from the inside out. In Jesus' Name,*
> *Amen.*

If you sincerely prayed that prayer in faith, the very Spirit of God lives in you forever! He now wants to help you grow in your relationship with Him.

Chapter Two The Essential, Overlooked Ingredient to More of the Spirit

1. *The New York Times*, August 19, 2012, *Why Waiting Is Torture*, by Alex Stone.
2. V. Raymond Edman, *They Found the Secret*, (Nashville: Zondervan Publishing, 1984), 74–75.

Chapter Four A Closed Mouth and a Yellow Pad

1. Some of these questions are found in Brad Jersak's book, *Can You Hear Me?* (Abbotsford, BC: Fresh Wind Press, 2003), 63–64.

Chapter Five Is That Really You, God?

1. For a more detailed explanation of how to engage in Scripture, see chapter 7 of my previous book, *Good News for Those Trying Harder*, (Colorado Springs: David C. Cook, 2008).
2. Tom Doyle, *Dreams and Visions*, (Nashville: Thomas Nelson Inc, 2012).
3. Jack Deere, *The Beginner's Guide to the Gift of Prophecy* (Kindle version , 2008), retrieved from www.amazon. com, chapter 3.

Chapter Six Hearing the Spirit for Others

1. I have been significantly influenced by Wayne Grudem's writing on this subject. For a more detailed explanation of prophecy, see *Systematic Theology*, by Wayne Grudem, (Nashville: Zondervan, 1984), 1049-1061.

Chapter Seven How to Share a Prophetic Word ...
Without Being Weird

1. Deere, Ibid., chapter 4
2. I learned this model from a dear friend, Arthur Ellison, who taught it in a seminar I attended.

Chapter Eight The Spirit of Healing

1. *Christianizing the Roman Empire: A.D. 100-400* (New Haven and London: Yale University Press, 1984) 22.
2. Ibid., 56–57
3. Ken Blue, *Authority to Heal*, (Downers Grove: InterVarsity Press, 1987) 25.

Chapter Nine How to Pray For the Sick

1. Neil Anderson, *The Bondage Breaker: Overcoming Negative Thoughts, Irrational Feelings, Habitual Sins,* (Eugene, OR: Harvest House Publishers, 2006)
2. Blue, Ibid., 103.
3. This model is an adapted version of the printed material of the three people I have learned the most from in this area—John Wimber, Ken Blue, and Michael Evans.

Chapter Ten How the Spirit Can Energize Your Prayer Life

1. I adapted this from *Building a Discipling Culture,* by Mike Breen and Steve Cockran, 2009 (Kindle version), retrieved from www.amazon.com. Discussed in chapter 11. My friend Bruce Hoppe designed the actual image.
2. Adapted from Wayne Grudem's definition, found in *Systematic Theology,* (Nashville: Zondervan Press, 1994,) 1070.
3. I now realize that had God given me this gift while in seminary, I wouldn't have been able to get a job at my current church, because my résumé would have been thrown out. At that time, the district superintendent was discarding the résumés of anyone who said they had a prayer language. So God has His purposes and His timing.

Chapter Eleven Are You Spirit-Filled?

1. Ann Voskamp, *One Thousand Gifts Devotional: Reflections on Finding Everyday Graces,* (Nashville: Zondervan, 2012), 9.

Chapter Twelve When the Spirit Comes in Power

1. If you are interested in reading more about my journey out of this performance-based Christianity, I talk about it in detail in my previous book, *Good News for Those Trying Harder, (Colorado Springs: David C. Cook, 2008).*

2. Edman, Ibid., 75.

3. As quoted by John Ortberg, *Faith and Doubt* (Nashville: Zondervan, 2008), 69–70.

4. Edman, Ibid., 43.

5. John White, *When the Spirit Comes with Power,* (Downers Grove: Intervarsity Press, 1988), 43.

6. Dr. E. A. Halleen, *The Golden Jubilee Book of the Swedish Evangelical Free Church,* 1934. Quoted in *The Diamond Jubilee Story of the Evangelical Free Church of America,* Minneapolis, MN: Free Church Publications, 1959, 140-141.

7. Martyn Lloyd-Jones, *Joy Unspeakable,* (Chicago: Harold Shaw Publishers, 2000), 61.